**1st EDITION**

# Perspectives on Diseases and Disorders

## Anorexia and Bulimia

Arthur Gillard
*Book Editor*

PERSPECTIVES
On Diseases & Disorders

GALE
CENGAGE Learning·

Detroit • New York • San Francisco • New Haven, Conn • Waterville, Maine • London

Elizabeth Des Chenes, *Director, Publishing Solutions*

© 2013 Greenhaven Press, a part of Gale, Cengage Learning

Gale and Greenhaven Press are registered trademarks used herein under license.

*For more information, contact:*
Greenhaven Press
27500 Drake Rd.
Farmington Hills, MI 48331-3535
Or you can visit our Internet site at gale.cengage.com

For product information and technology assistance, contact us at

Gale Customer Support, 1-800-877-4253
For permission to use material from this text or product, submit all requests online at www.cengage.com/permissions

Further permissions questions can be e-mailed to permissionrequest@cengage.com

Articles in Greenhaven Press anthologies are often edited for length to meet page requirements. In addition, original titles of these works are changed to clearly present the main thesis and to explicitly indicate the author's opinion. Every effort is made to ensure that Greenhaven Press accurately reflects the original intent of the authors. Every effort has been made to trace the owners of copyrighted material.

Cover image © Caro/Alamy.

**LIBRARY OF CONGRESS CATALOGING-IN-PUBLICATION DATA**

Anorexia and bulimia / Arthur Gillard, book editor.
    pages cm. -- (Perspectives on diseases and disorders)
  Includes bibliographical references and index.
  ISBN 978-0-7377-6348-5 (hardcover)
 1. Anorexia nervosa. 2. Bulimia. I. Gillard, Arthur, editor of compilation.
  RC552.A5A548 2013
  616.85'262--dc23
                                                          2012042414

Printed in the United States of America
1 2 3 4 5 6 7 17 16 15 14 13

# CONTENTS

**CHAPTER 3**    Personal Experiences with Anorexia
and Bulimia

# FOREWORD

*"Medicine, to produce health, has to examine disease."*
—Plutarch

Independent research on a health issue is often the first step to complement discussions with a physician. But locating accurate, well-organized, understandable medical information can be a challenge. A simple Internet search on terms such as "cancer" or "diabetes," for example, returns an intimidating number of results. Sifting through the results can be daunting, particularly when some of the information is inconsistent or even contradictory. The Greenhaven Press series Perspectives on Diseases and Disorders offers a solution to the often overwhelming nature of researching diseases and disorders.

From the clinical to the personal, titles in the Perspectives on Diseases and Disorders series provide students and other researchers with authoritative, accessible information in unique anthologies that include basic information about the disease or disorder, controversial aspects of diagnosis and treatment, and first-person accounts of those impacted by the disease. The result is a well-rounded combination of primary and secondary sources that, together, provide the reader with a better understanding of the disease or disorder.

Each volume in Perspectives on Diseases and Disorders explores a particular disease or disorder in detail. Material for each volume is carefully selected from a wide range of sources, including encyclopedias, journals, newspapers, non-fiction books, speeches, government documents, pamphlets, organization newsletters, and position papers. Articles in the first chapter provide an authoritative, up-to-date overview that covers symptoms, causes and effects, treatments, cures, and medical advances. The second chapter presents a substantial number of opposing viewpoints on controversial treatments and other current debates relating to the volume topic. The third chapter offers a variety of personal perspectives on the disease or disorder. Patients, doctors, caregivers, and loved ones represent just some of the voices found in this narrative chapter.

Each Perspectives on Diseases and Disorders volume also includes:

- An **annotated table of contents** that provides a brief summary of each article in the volume.
- An **introduction** specific to the volume topic.
- Full-color **charts and graphs** to illustrate key points, concepts, and theories.
- Full-color **photos** that show aspects of the disease or disorder and enhance textual material.
- **"Fast Facts"** that highlight pertinent additional statistics and surprising points.
- A **glossary** providing users with definitions of important terms.
- A **chronology** of important dates relating to the disease or disorder.
- An annotated list of **organizations to contact** for students and other readers seeking additional information.
- A **bibliography** of additional books and periodicals for further research.
- A detailed **subject index** that allows readers to quickly find the information they need.

Whether a student researching a disorder, a patient recently diagnosed with a disease, or an individual who simply wants to learn more about a particular disease or disorder, a reader who turns to Perspectives on Diseases and Disorders will find a wealth of information in each volume that offers not only basic information, but also vigorous debate from multiple perspectives.

# INTRODUCTION

Anorexia and bulimia are eating disorders that involve dissatisfaction with one's body and a preoccupation with losing weight. Techniques used to lose weight fall into two general categories: restricting calorie intake (i.e., eating little) and purging the body of excess calories via such techniques as self-induced vomiting, excessive exercise, and inappropriate use of laxatives, enemas, or diuretics. All of these techniques take a considerable toll on the body, making eating disorders the most harmful and deadly of the mental disorders.

Despite the popular conception that anorexics do not eat, and bulimics always vomit, there is considerable overlap between the two disorders; although one difference between the two conditions is that bulimics tend to be of normal weight or even overweight, whereas in order to be diagnosed with anorexia someone must be considerably below the lowest healthy weight for their height. In any case, it is not uncommon for someone to alternate between the two, or to initially be anorexic and later develop bulimia.

An eating disorder is a bewildering and harrowing experience. One parent of an eating-disordered youth described it as an "alien force taking charge of my child's eating."[1] As the authors of *Surviving an Eating Disorder: Strategies for Families and Friends* note, "It's difficult to fully comprehend the nightmare of living with an eating disorder. It is heartbreaking to hear a lovely 15-year-old girl say, 'I know that this could kill me. I would just rather be dead than fat.' Then there was 13-year-old Jamie who said, 'It's not just a glass of milk. It is liquid with calories and that is about as terrifying as it gets.'"[2]

A common misconception is that anorexics do not experience hunger; typically they are hungry all the time and think about food constantly but are incapable of allowing themselves to satisfy their hunger. After a prolonged period of denying such a primal drive as hunger, the capacity for self-regulation can be lost, leading to extreme bingeing and purging behavior. As one eating disorder patient put it,

> After years of starvation, my body cried out so urgently for food that I gave in . . . and started a cycle of bingeing. I ate and ate until I couldn't eat any more, until my stomach hurt. I ate entire boxes of cookies, loaves of bread, a half-gallon of ice cream—anything I could get my hands on. Then the anxiety set in. I remember thinking, What have I just done? I have absolutely no willpower. That was when I had to vomit.[3]

The understanding of anorexia, bulimia, and related eating disorders has evolved over time. At one time the cause of eating disorders was thought to be purely physical—e.g., anorexia was thought to be a form of tuberculosis, a result of hormone imbalances, or an endocrine deficiency. In the 1930s emotional and psychological issues began to be seriously considered by the medical community as being at least partly involved in causing these illnesses; the case study of Ellen West, a patient of Swiss psychiatrist Ludwig Binswanger from 1930 to 1933, was one of the first to seriously consider the interior perspective of a patient suffering from an eating disorder. His written accounts used her poetry and excerpts from her diary to illustrate her emotions and psychological state.

Recently much attention has focused on the influence of culture and the media, particularly following a number of high-profile deaths of anorexic fashion models, as well as studies suggesting a link between body dissatisfaction/disordered eating and pervasive media images of very thin models and actresses. But while some of those who study eating disorders put primary blame on cultural influences, others point out that while many people (particularly women) suffer from disordered eating at some point in their lives, only a small percentage suffer from anorexia and bulimia.

Advances in science and technology in recent decades are yielding a wealth of information on physical correlates of anorexia and bulimia. For example, using an advanced brain scanning technique called functional magnetic resonance imaging (fMRI), researchers at the University of California–San Diego Medical Center have

An eating disorder is a bewildering and scary experience. One parent describes it as an "alien force taking charge of my child's eating." (© Angela Hampton Picture Library/ Alamy)

discovered differences in the brains of anorectic patients in regions involved in processing taste, regulating emotion and reward, and interpreting internal bodily signals. In another study using fMRI, Rachel Marsh of Columbia University and her colleagues found that bulimics had less activity in regions of the brain associated with self-regulation and impulse control.

Genetic research suggests that people can inherit tendencies to develop eating disorders. According to eating-disorder experts Pamela Carlton and Deborah Ashin, someone with bulimic or anorectic relatives are seven to twelve times more likely to develop an eating disorder than the general population, although the authors note that "this doesn't mean that you can 'inherit' an eating disorder, but you can have a genetic make-up that increases your chance of developing one."[4] As author Sheila Himmel, whose daughter suffered from both anorexia and bulimia, puts it, "The rule you often hear about eating disorders is 'Genetics loads the gun, and experience/cultural pressure/trauma pulls the trigger.'"[5]

Increasingly, approaches to these disorders have taken a more integral or comprehensive approach, attempting to address all the complex factors that may be involved, rather than looking for one simple cause. Carlton and Ashin note:

> Despite considerable research . . . the cause of eating disorders is still unknown. . . . What we do know is that developing an eating disorder is influenced by a combination of factors: psychological, developmental, social, cultural, genetic, and neurochemical (brain chemistry). Just one of these factors alone will not cause an eating disorder, but a combination of these elements can increase the possibility of developing one. Often, the lines between these different factors blur: for instance, personality traits are psychological as well as genetic; cultural influences and social pressures often overlap.[6]

It is important to understand that regardless of how an eating disorder gets started, it tends to develop its own momentum and become more seriously entrenched over time. Part of the reason for this is due to the effects on the brain of malnutrition and starvation, as illustrated by the famous Minnesota experiment done in World War II, in which a group of physically and psychologically healthy men voluntarily underwent severe calorie restriction for a prolonged period of time. As the experiment progressed, signs of physical, emotional, and cognitive deterioration became progressively more apparent, including depression, anxiety, hypersensitivity to light and noise, decreased tolerance for cold, social withdrawal, gastrointestinal discomfort, apathy, listlessness, and auditory and visual disturbances. The experiment suggests that "many of the symptoms that might have been thought to be specific to anorexia nervosa or bulimia are actually the result of starvation. These are not limited to food and weight, but extend to virtually all areas of psychological and social functioning."[7]

In 2009 the federal Agency for Healthcare Research and Quality reported that hospitalizations for eating disorders declined by 23 percent between 2007 and 2009. Some speculate that the drop is due to insurance companies' showing increased reluctance to pay for hospitalization for eating disorders, opting for other options, such as outpatient care. Other experts see it as a hopeful sign that progress is being made in treating anorexia and bulimia, with increased reliance on evidence-based therapy such as family-based treatment for anorexia and cognitive-behavioral therapy for bulimia. In addition, it is now known that getting treatment earlier in the course of an eating disorder greatly improves the chances of a successful outcome. Considered in that light, a report by the Agency for Healthcare Research and Quality that there has been a 119 percent increase in eating disorder hospitalizations among children aged twelve or younger between 1999 and

2006—which is taken by some as a discouraging sign that eating disorders are *affecting* people at younger ages—may instead be an indication that health-care providers are *detecting* these illnesses at younger ages, with greater prospects for a successful outcome.

*Perspectives on Diseases and Disorders: Anorexia and Bulimia* provides an accessible overview of a challenging disease. Incorporating the perspectives of experts, health-care providers, and anorexia/bulimia sufferers themselves, this volume provides opportunities to enhance awareness about these serious illnesses.

## Notes

1. Pamela Carlton and Deborah Ashin, *Take Charge of Your Child's Eating Disorder: A Physician's Step-by-Step Guide to Defeating Anorexia and Bulimia.* New York: Marlowe, 2007, p. 20.
2. Michele Siegel, Judith Brisman, and Margot Weinshel, *Surviving an Eating Disorder: Strategies for Families and Friends*, 3rd ed. New York: Collins Living, 2009, p. 50.
3. Judy Tam Sargent, *The Long Road Back: A Survivor's Guide to Anorexia.* Georgetown, MA: North Star, 1999, p. 33.
4. Carlton and Ashin, *Take Charge of your Child's Eating Disorder*, pp. 23–24.
5. Sheila Himmel and Lisa Himmel, *Hungry: A Mother and Daughter Fight Anorexia.* New York: Berkley, 2009, p. 5.
6. Carlton and Ashin, *Take Charge of Your Child's Eating Disorder*, p. 21.
7. Medusa, "Anorexia, Bulimia, & the Minnesota Starvation Experiment," August 10, 2009. www.2medusa .com/2009/08/anorexia-bulimia-minnesota-starva tion.html.

# CHAPTER 1

# Understanding Anorexia and Bulimia

# Anorexia Nervosa: An Overview

## Tish Davidson

Tish Davidson is a nonfiction author who writes primarily on medicine and biological science. She has a bachelor of science degree with a major in biology from the College of William and Mary and a master of arts in biology from Dartmouth College.

Anorexia nervosa is a potentially fatal psychiatric condition characterized by an irrational fear of gaining weight, a distorted body image, and self-starvation behaviors. Starvation is accomplished either via fasting (in the case of restricting-type anorexia) or via elimination of calories after eating by abuse of diuretics, enemas, laxatives, or self-induced vomiting (in the case of purge-type anorexia). Anorexia is believed to be caused by a complex interaction of biological, social, and psychological factors. It is diagnosed via a combination of medical and psychological tests, and treatment can include hospitalization, nutrition education, psychotherapy, psychiatric medication, and alternative treatments. Treatment is difficult, and a large percentage of patients never fully recover.

*Photo on facing page. Bulimia nervosa is a potentially life-threatening eating disorder that involves repeated binge eating followed by purging to avoid gaining weight.* (© **Leila Cutler/Alamy**)

**SOURCE:** Tish Davidson, "Anorexia Nervosa," *The Gale Encyclopedia of Medicine,* ed. Laurie J. Fundukian, vol. 1, Gale, 2011, pp. 265–270. Copyright © 2011 Cengage Learning.

Anorexia nervosa is a psychiatric disorder characterized by an unrealistic fear of weight gain, self-starvation, and conspicuous distortion of body image. The individual is obsessed with becoming increasingly thinner and limits food intake to the point where health is compromised. The disorder can be fatal. The name comes from two Latin words that mean nervous inability to eat.

Anorexia is a disorder of industrialized countries where food is abundant and the culture values a thin appearance. About 1% of Americans are anorectic and female anorectics outnumber males 10:1. In men the disorder is more often diagnosed in homosexuals than in heterosexuals. Some experts believe that number of diagnosed anorectics represents only the most severe cases, and that many more people have anorexic tendencies, but their symptoms do not rise to the level needed for a medical diagnosis.

Anorexia has been characterized as a "rich white girl" disorder. Most anorectics are white, and about three-quarters of them come from households at the middle income level or above. However, in the 2000s, the number of blacks and Hispanics diagnosed with anorexia has increased.

Anorexia can occur in people as young as age 7. However, the disorder most often begins during adolescence. It is most likely to start at one of two times, either age 14 or 18. Interestingly, this corresponds with the age of transitioning into and out of high school. There is a secondary peak of individuals who become anorexic in their 40s. The younger the age at which anorexic behavior starts, the more difficult it is to cure. Preteens who develop anorexia often show signs of compulsive behavior and depression in addition to anorexia.

## Characteristics of Anorectics

Anorexia is often thought of as a modern problem, but the English physician Richard Morton first described it in 1689. In the twenty-first century anorexia nervosa is recognized as a psychiatric disorder in the *Diagnostic and Statistical Manual for Mental Disorders Fourth Edition (DSM-IV-TR)* published by the American Psychiatric Association.

Individuals with anorexia are on an irrational, unrelenting quest to lose weight, and no matter how much they lose and how much their health is compromised, they want to lose more weight. Recognizing the development of anorexia can be difficult, especially in a society that values and glamorizes thinness. Dieting is often the trigger that starts a person down the road to anorexia. The future anorectic may begin by skipping meals or taking only tiny portions. She (most anorectics are female) always has an excuse for why she does not want to eat. . . . She also begins to read food labels and knows exactly how many calories and how much fat are in everything she eats. Many anorectics practically eliminate fat and sugar from their diets and seem to live on diet soda and lettuce. Some future anorectics begin to exercise compulsively to burn extra calories. Eventually these practices have serious health consequences. At some point, the line between problem eating and an eating disorder is crossed.

Anorectics spend a lot of time looking in the mirror, obsessing about clothing size, and practicing negative self-talk about their bodies. Some are secretive about eating and will avoid eating in front of other people. They may develop strange eating habits such as chewing their food and then spitting it out, or they may have rigid ideas about "good" and "bad" food. Anorectics will lie about their eating habits and their weight to friends, family, and healthcare providers. Many anorectics experience depression and anxiety disorders.

There are two major subtypes of anorectics. Restrictive anorectics control their weight by rigorously limiting the amount of calories they eat or by fasting. They may exercise excessively or abuse drugs or herbal remedies

Anorexia nervosa is a psychiatric disorder characterized by an unrealistic fear of weight gain, self-starvation, and conspicuous distortion of body image. (© Oscar Burriel/Photo Researchers, Inc.)

[that] claim to increase the rate at which the body burns calories. Purge-type anorectics eat and then get rid of the calories and weight by self-induced vomiting, excessive laxative use, and abuse of diuretics or enemas.

Competitive athletes of all races have an increased risk of developing anorexia nervosa, especially in sports where weight is tied to performance. Jockeys, wrestlers, figure skaters, cross-country runners, and gymnasts (especially female gymnasts) have higher than average rates of anorexia. People such as actors, models, cheerleaders, and dancers (especially ballet dancers) who are judged mainly on their appearance are also at high risk of developing the disorder.

## Causes and Symptoms

Anorexia is a complex disorder that does not have a single cause but appears to result from the interaction of cultural and biological factors. Research suggests that some people have a predisposition toward anorexia and that something then triggers the behavior, which then becomes self-reinforcing. Hereditary, biological, psychological and social factors all appear to play a role.

While the precise cause of the disorder is not known, it has been linked to the following:

- *Heredity*. Twin studies show that if one twin has anorexia nervosa, the other has a greater likelihood of developing the disorder. Having a close relative, usually a mother or a sister, with anorexia nervosa also increases the likelihood of other (usually female) family members developing the disorder. However, when compared to many other diseases, the inherited component of anorexia nervosa appears to be fairly small.
- *Biological factors*. There is some evidence that anorexia nervosa is linked to abnormal neurotransmitter activity in the part of the brain that controls pleasure and appetite. Neurotransmitters are also involved in other mental disorders such as depression. Research in this area is relatively new and the findings are unclear. People with anorexia tend to feel full sooner than other people. Some researchers believe that this is related to the fact that [the] stomach of people with anorexia tends to empty more slowly than normal; others think it may be related to the appetite control mechanism of the brain.

• *Psychological factors.* Certain personality types appear to be more vulnerable to developing anorexia nervosa. Anorectics tend to be perfectionists who have unrealistic expectations about how they "should" look and perform. They tend to have a black-or-white, right-or-wrong, all-or-nothing way of seeing situations. Many anorectics lack a strong sense of identity and instead take their identity from pleasing others. Virtually all anorectics have low-self worth. Many experience depression and anxiety disorders, although researchers do not know if this is a cause or a result of the eating disorder.

• *Social factors.* Anorectics are more likely to come either from overprotective families or disordered families where there is a lot of conflict and inconsistency. Either way, the anorectic feels a need to be in control of something, and that something becomes body weight. The family often has high, sometimes unrealistic and rigid, expectations. Often something stressful or upsetting triggers the start of anorexic behaviors. This may be as simple as a family member teasing about the person's weight, nagging about eating junk food, commenting on how clothes fit, or comparing the person unfavorably to someone who is thin. Life events such as moving, starting a new school, breaking up with a boyfriend, or even entering puberty and feeling awkward about one's changing body can trigger anorexic behavior. Overlaying the family situation is the unrelenting media message that thin is good and fat is bad; thin people are successful, glamorous, and happy, fat people are stupid, lazy, and failures.

Although anorexia nervosa is still considered a disorder that largely affects women, its incidence in the male population is rising. Less is known about the causes of anorexia in males, but some risk factors are the same as for females. These include certain occupational goals (e.g., jockey) and increasing media emphasis on external appearance in men. Moreover, homosexual males are under pressure to conform to an ideal body weight that is about 20 pounds lighter than the standard "attractive" weight for heterosexual males.

## Signs and Symptoms

Anorexic behavior has physical and psychological consequences. These include:

- excessive weight loss; loss of muscle
- stunted growth and delayed sexual maturation in preteens
- gastrointestinal complications: liver damage, diarrhea, constipation, bloating, stomach pain
- cardiovascular complications: irregular heartbeat, low pulse rate, cardiac arrest
- urinary system complications: kidney damage, kidney failure, incontinence, urinary tract infections
- skeletal system complications: loss of bone mass, increased risk of fractures, teeth eroded by stomach acid from repeat vomiting
- reproductive system complications (women): irregular menstrual periods, amenorhhea, infertility
- reproductive system complications (men): loss of sex drive, infertility
- fatigue, irritation, headaches, depression, anxiety, impaired judgment and thinking
- fainting, seizures, low blood sugar
- chronically cold hands and feet
- weakened immune system, swollen glands, increased susceptibility to infections
- development of fine hair called lanugo on the shoulders, back, arms, and face; head hair loss; blotchy, dry skin
- potentially life-threatening electrolyte imbalances
- coma
- increased risk of self-mutilation (cutting)
- increased risk of suicide
- death

## Diagnosis Is Based on Various Evaluations

Diagnosis of anorexia nervosa is made when the individual meets the criteria for the disorder outlined in the *DSM IV-TR*.

Anorexia is diagnosed when most of the following conditions are present:

- an overriding obsession with food and thinness that controls activities and eating patterns every hour of every day
- the individual weighs less than 85% of the average weight for his or her age and height group and willfully and intentionally refuses to maintain an appropriate body weight
- extreme fear of gaining weight or becoming fat, even when the individual is significantly underweight
- a distorted self-image that fuels a refusal to admit to being underweight, even when this is demonstrably true
- refusal to admit that being severely underweight is dangerous to health
- for women, three missed menstrual periods in a row after menstruation has been established

Diagnosis is based on several factors including a patient history, physical examination, laboratory tests, and a mental status evaluation. A patient history is less helpful in diagnosing anorexia than in diagnosing many diseases because many people with anorexia lie repeatedly about how much they eat and their use of laxatives, enemas, and medications. The patient may, however, complain about related symptoms such as fatigue, headaches, dizziness, constipation, or frequent infections.

A physical examination begins with weight and blood pressure and moves through all the signs listed above. Based on the physical exam, the physician will order laboratory tests. In general these tests will include a complete blood count (CBC), urinalysis, blood chemistries (to determine electrolyte levels), and liver function tests. The physician may also order an electrocardiogram to look for heart abnormalities. Other conditions . . . can cause weight loss or vomiting after eating. . . . The physician may perform tests needed to rule out the presence of these disorders and assess the patient's nutritional status.

The individual may be referred to a psychiatrist for a mental status evaluation. The psychiatrist will evaluate things such as whether the person is oriented in time and space, appearance, observable state of emotion (affect), attitude toward food and weight, delusional thinking, and thoughts of self-harm or suicide. This evaluation helps to distinguish between anorexia and other psychiatric disorders, including depression, schizophrenia, social phobia, obsessive-compulsive disorder, and body dysmorphic disorder. Two diagnostic tests that are often used are the Eating Attitudes Test (EAT) and the Eating Disorder Inventory (EDI).

> ## FAST FACT
>
> According to a study published in the *Archives of General Psychiatry* in 2011, the mortality rate of anorexics is twice that of schizophrenics and three times as high as those with bipolar disorder.

## Traditional Treatment

Treatment choices depend on the degree to which anorexic behavior has resulted in physical damage and whether the person is a danger to him or herself. Medical treatment should be supplemented with psychiatric treatment. Patients are frequently uncooperative and resist treatment, denying that their life may be endangered and insisting that the doctor only wants to "make them get fat."

Hospitalization is recommended for anorexics with any of the following characteristics:

- weight of 40% or more below normal; or weight loss over a three-month period of more than 30 pounds
- severely disturbed metabolism
- severe binging and purging

• signs of psychosis
• severe depression or risk of suicide
• family in crisis

Hospital inpatient care is first geared toward correcting problems that present as immediate medical crises, such as severe malnutrition, severe electrolyte imbalance, irregular heart beat, pulse below 45 beats per minute, or low body temperature. Patients are hospitalized if they are a high suicide risk, have severe clinical depression, or exhibit signs of an altered mental state. They may also need to be hospitalized to interrupt weight loss, stop the cycle of vomiting, exercising and/or laxative abuse, treat substance disorders, or for additional medical evaluation.

Day treatment or partial hospitalization where the patient goes every day to an extensive treatment program provides structured mealtimes, nutrition education, intensive therapy, medical monitoring, and supervision. If day treatment fails, the patient may need to be hospitalized or enter a full-time residential treatment facility.

Anorexia nervosa is a chronic disease and relapses are common and to be expected. Outpatient treatment provides medical supervision, nutrition counseling, self-help strategies, and therapy after the patient has reached some weight goals and shows stability.

A nutrition consultant or dietitian is an essential part of the team needed to successfully treat anorexia. The first treatment concern is to get the individual medically stable by increasing calorie intake and balancing electrolytes. After that, nutritional therapy is needed [to] support the long process of recovery and stable weight gain. This is an intensive process involving nutrition education, meal planning, nutrition monitoring, and helping the anorectic develop a healthy relationship with food.

## Psychotherapy, Drugs, and Alternative Treatment

Medical intervention helps alleviate the immediate physical problems associated with anorexia, but by itself, it rarely changes behavior. Psychotherapy plays a major role in helping the anorectic understand and recover from anorexia. Several different types of psychotherapy are used depending on the individual's situation. Generally, the goal of psychotherapy is [to] help the individual develop a healthy attitude toward their body and food. This may involve addressing the root causes of anorexic behavior as well as addressing the behavior itself. . . .

Anorectics are treated with a variety of medications to address physical problems brought about by their eating

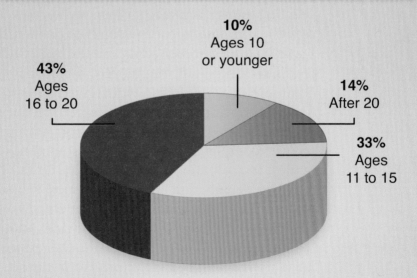

**The Age of Onset of Anorexia Nervosa**

10%
Ages 10 or younger

14%
After 20

43%
Ages
16 to 20

33%
Ages
11 to 15

Data derived from the National Association of Anorexia Nervosa and Associated Disorders.

Taken from: Martha Irvine. "'Ana' Brings Anorexia to Life." *The Free Lance—Star*, June 5, 2005.

disorder and to treat additional psychiatric problems such as depression, anxiety, and suicidal thoughts. The medications used will vary depending on the individual, however, depression is common among anorectics and is often treated with antidepressant drugs.

Alternative treatments should serve as complementary to a conventional treatment program. Alternative therapies for anorexia nervosa include diet and nutrition counseling, herbal therapy, hydrotherapy, aromatherapy, Ayurvedic medicine [holistic alternative treatments developed in India], and mind/body medicine. . . .

## The Prognosis Is Complicated

Anorexia nervosa is difficult to treat successfully. Medical stabilization, nutrition therapy, continued medical monitoring, and substantial psychiatric treatment give a person with anorexia the best chance of recovery. Estimates suggest that between 20% and 30% of people in treatment drop out too soon and have major relapses. Even those who stay in treatment relapse occasionally. Treating anorexia is often a long, slow, frustrating process that can cost many thousands of dollars. The earlier in life that the disorder starts and the longer the disorder continues untreated, the more difficult it is [to] bring about recovery. Many individuals with anorexia are willfully uncooperative and do not want to recover.

About half the people treated for anorexia nervosa recover completely and are able (sometimes with difficulty) to maintain a normal weight. Of the remaining 50% between 6% and 20% die. The most frequent causes of death associated with anorexia are starvation, electrolyte imbalance, heart failure, and suicide. About 20% remain dangerously underweight, and the rest remain thin. Long-term health complications are common.

# Bulimia Nervosa: An Overview

## Tish Davidson

Tish Davidson is a nonfiction author who writes primarily on medicine and biological science. She has a bachelor of science degree with a major in biology from the College of William and Mary and a master of arts in biology from Dartmouth College.

Bulimia nervosa is a serious eating disorder characterized by fear of weight gain and a distorted body image. Bulimics go through a repetitive cycle of binge eating, in which a large amount of food is consumed, followed by purging via such techniques as self-induced vomiting, laxatives, enemas, or diuretics. Bulimics tend to have poor impulse control and to engage in risky behavior. More than half of bulimics have a history of anorexia, and some anorexics purge. A person with an eating disorder may also alternate between bulimic and anorexic behavior. A combination of medical and psychiatric tests are used to diagnose bulimia. Treatment options include hospitalization, psychiatric medication, psychotherapy, and nutritional counseling.

**SOURCE:** Tish Davidson, "Bulimia Nervosa," *The Gale Encyclopedia of Medicine,* ed. Laurie J. Fundukian, vol. 1, Gale, 2011, pp. 788–795. Copyright © 2011 Cengage Learning.

Bulimia nervosa is a potentially life-threatening eating disorder that involves repeated binge eating followed by purging the body of calories to avoid gaining weight. The person who has bulimia has an irrational fear of gaining weight and a distorted body image. Bulimia nervosa can have potentially fatal health consequences.

Bulimia nervosa is primarily a disorder of industrialized countries where food is abundant and the culture values a thin appearance. In Westernized countries, the rate of bulimia has been increasing since the 1950s. Bulimia is the most common eating disorder in the United States. Overall, about 3% of Americans are bulimic. Of these, 85%–90% are female. The rate is highest among adolescents and college women, averaging 5%–6%. In men, the disorder is more often diagnosed in homosexuals than in heterosexuals. Some experts believe that the number of diagnosed bulimics represents only the most severe cases and that many more people have bulimic tendencies but are successful in hiding their symptoms. In one study, 40% of college women reported isolated incidents of bingeing and purging.

Bulimia affects people from all racial, ethnic, and socioeconomic groups. The disorder usually begins later in life than anorexia nervosa. Most people begin bingeing and purging in their late teens through their twenties. Men tend to start at an older age than women. About 5% of people with bulimia begin the behavior after age 25. Bulimia is uncommon in children under age 14.

## The Characteristics of a Bulimic

Bulimia is an eating disorder whose main feature is eating an unreasonably large amount of food in a short time and then following this binge by purging the body of calories. Purging most often is done by self-induced vomiting, but it can also be done by laxative, enema, or diuretic abuse. Alternately, some people with bulimia do not purge but use extreme exercising and post-binge fasting to burn calories. Nonpurging bulimia is sometimes called exercise bulimia. Bulimia nervosa is officially recognized as a psychiatric disorder in the *Diagnostic and Statistical Manual for Mental Disorders Fourth Edition, Text Revision (DSM-IV-TR)* published by the American Psychiatric Association.

Many people with bulimia will consume 3,000–10,000 calories in an hour. For example, they will start out intending to eat one slice of cake and end up eating the entire cake. One distinguishing aspect of bulimia is how out of control people with bulimia feel when they are eating. They will eat and eat, continuing even when they feel full and become uncomfortable.

Most people with bulimia recognize that their behavior is not normal; they simply cannot control it. They usually feel ashamed and guilty over their binge/purge habits. As a result, they frequently become secretive about their eating and purging. They may, for example, eat at night after the family has gone to bed or buy food at the grocery store and eat it in the car before going home. Many bulimics choose high-fat, high-sugar foods that are easy to eat and easy to regurgitate. They become adept at inducing vomiting, usually by sticking a finger down their throat and triggering the gag reflex. After a while, they can vomit at will. Repeated purging has serious physical and emotional consequences.

Many individuals with bulimia are of normal weight, and a fair number of men who become bulimic were overweight as children. This makes it difficult for family and friends to recognize someone suffering from this disorder. People with bulimia often lie about induced vomiting and laxative abuse, although they may complain of symptoms related to their binge/purge cycles and seek medical help for those problems. People with bulimia tend to be more impulsive than people with other eating disorders. Lack of impulse control often leads to risky sexual behavior, anger management problems, and alcohol and drug abuse.

## The Overlap with Anorexia Nervosa

A subset of people with bulimia also have anorexia nervosa. Anorexia nervosa is an eating disorder that involves self-imposed starvation. These people often purge after eating only a small or a normal sized portion of food. Some studies have shown that up to 60% of people with bulimia have a history of anorexia nervosa. Some people are primarily anorexic and severely restrict their calorie intake while also purging the small amounts they do eat. Others move back and forth between anorectic and bulimic behaviors.

Dieting usually is the trigger that starts a person down the road to bulimia. The cycle might begin with a person going on a rigorous low-calorie diet. Unable to stick with the unrealistic diet, he or she then overeats, feels guilty about overeating, and then exercises or purges to get rid of the unwanted calories. At first this may happen only occasionally, but gradually these sessions of bingeing and purging become routine and start to intrude on the person's friendships, daily activities, and health. Eventually these practices have serious physical and emotional consequences that need to be addressed by healthcare professionals.

Competitive athletes have an increased risk of developing bulimia nervosa, especially in sports where weight is tied to performance and where a low percentage of body fat is highly desirable. Jockeys, wrestlers, bodybuilders, figure skaters, cross-country runners, and gymnasts have higher than average rates of bulimia. People such as actors, models, cheerleaders, and dancers who are judged mainly on their appearance are also at high risk of developing the disorder. . . .

## FAST FACT

A study of seventeen bulimics published in the *American Journal of Psychiatry* in 1993 reports that after purging, over a thousand calories from the prior binge were still retained in the body.

## Causes and Symptoms

Bulimia nervosa is a complex disorder that does not have a single cause. Research suggests that some people have a predisposition toward bulimia and that some catalyst then triggers the behavior, which then becomes self-reinforcing. Hereditary, biological, psychological and social factors all appear to play a role.

- *Heredity:* Twin studies suggest that there is an inherited component to bulimia nervosa but that it is small. Having a close relative, usually a mother or a sister, with bulimia slightly increases the likelihood of other (usually female) family members developing the disorder. However, when compared with other inherited diseases or even to anorexia nervosa, the genetic contribution to developing this disorder appears less important than many other factors. Family history of depression, alcoholism, and obesity also increase the risk of developing bulimia.

- *Biological factors:* There is some evidence that bulimia is linked [to] low levels of serotonin in the brain. Serotonin is a neurotransmitter. One of its functions is to help regulate the feeling of fullness or satiety that tells a person to stop eating. Neurotransmitters are also involved in other mental disorders that often occur with bulimia such as depression. Other research suggests that people with bulimia may have abnormal levels of leptin, a protein that helps regulate weight by telling the body to take in less food. Research in this area is relatively new, and the findings are still unclear.

- *Psychological factors:* Certain personality types appear to be more vulnerable to developing bulimia. People with bulimia tend to have poor impulse control. They are often involved in risky behaviors such as shoplifting, drug or alcohol abuse, and risky sexual activities. People with bulimia might have low self-worth and depend on the approval of others to feel good about themselves. They are aware that their behavior is abnormal. After a binge/purge session, they are ashamed and vow never to repeat the cycle, but the next time they are unable to control the impulse to eat and purge. They also tend to have a black-or-white, all-or-nothing way of seeing situations. Major depression, obsessive-compulsive disorder, and anxiety disorders are more common among individuals who are bulimic.

- *Social factors*: The families of people who develop bulimia are more likely to have members who have problems with alcoholism, depression, and obesity. These families also tend to have a high level of open conflict and disordered, unpredictable lives. Often something stressful or upsetting triggers the urge to diet stringently and then begin binge/purge behaviors. This may be as simple as a family member teasing about the person's weight, nagging about eating junk food, commenting on how clothes fit, or comparing the person unfavorably to someone who is thin. Life events such as moving, starting a new school, and breaking up with a boyfriend can also trigger binge/purge behavior. Overlaying the family situation is the false but unrelenting media message that thin is "good" and fat is "bad."

## Signs and Symptoms

People with bulimia are very good at hiding their behavior, and weight, heart rate, and blood pressure may all be normal. However, binge/purge cycles have physical consequences. These include:

- teeth damaged from repeated exposure to stomach acid from vomiting; eroded tooth enamel
- swollen salivary glands; sores in mouth and throat
- dehydration
- sores or calluses on knuckles or hands from using them to induce vomiting

- electrolyte imbalances revealed by laboratory tests
- dry skin
- fatigue
- irregular or absent menstrual cycles in women

## Diagnosis Involves Diverse Evaluations

Diagnosis is based on several factors including a patient history, physical examination, the results of laboratory tests, and a mental status evaluation. A patient history is less helpful in diagnosing bulimia than in diagnosing many diseases because many people with bulimia lie about their

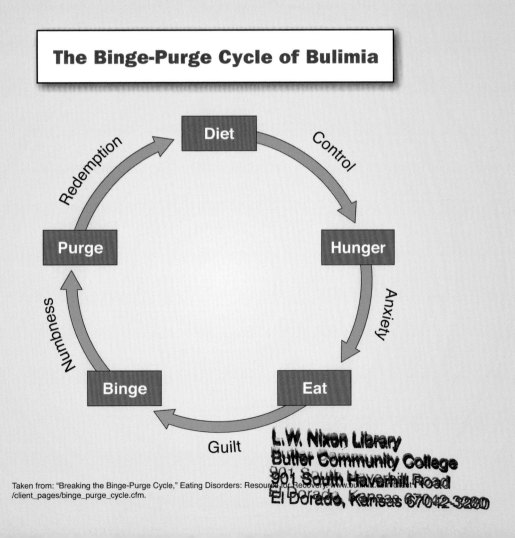

**The Binge-Purge Cycle of Bulimia**

Diet
Control
Hunger
Anxiety
Eat
Guilt
Binge
Numbness
Purge
Redemption

Taken from: "Breaking the Binge-Purge Cycle," Eating Disorders: Resources for Recovery, www.bulimia.com/client_pages/binge_purge_cycle.cfm.

bingeing and purging and their use of laxatives, enemas, and medications. The patient may, however, complain about related symptoms such as fatigue or feeling bloated. Many people with bulimia express extreme concern about their weight during the examination.

A physical examination begins with weight and blood pressure and moves through the body looking for the signs listed above. Based on the physical exam and patient history, the physician will order laboratory tests. In general, these tests will include a complete blood count (CBC), urinalysis, and blood chemistries (to determine electrolyte levels). People suspected of being exercise bulimic may need to have x rays to look for damage to bones from overexercising.

Several different evaluations can be used to examine a person's mental state. Psychiatric assessment usually includes four components:

- a thorough history of body weight, eating patterns, diets, typical daily food intake, methods of purging (if used), and concept of ideal weight
- a history of the patient's significant relationships with parents, siblings, and peers, including present or past physical, emotional, or sexual abuse
- a history of previous psychiatric treatment (if any) and assessment of comorbid (occurring at the same time as the bulimia) mood, anxiety, substance abuse, or personality disorders
- administration of standardized instruments that measure attitudes toward eating, body size, and weight; common tests for eating disorders include the Eating Disorder Examination, the Eating Disorder Inventory, the Eating Attitude Test (EAT), and the Kids' Eating Disorder Survey (KEDS).

Once all information has been compiled, bulimia nervosa is diagnosed when most of the following conditions are present:

- Repeated episodes of binge eating followed by behavior to compensate for the binge (i.e., purging, fasting, over-exercising). Binge eating is defined as eating a significantly larger amount of food in a limited time than most people typically would eat.
- Binge/purge episodes occur at least twice a week for a period of three or more months.
- The individual feels unable to control or stop an eating binge once it starts and will continue to eat even if uncomfortably full.
- The individual is overly concerned about body weight and shape and puts unreasonable emphasis on physical appearance when evaluating his or her self-worth.
- Bingeing and purging does not occur exclusively during periods of anorexia nervosa.

## Treatment May Be Multifaceted

Treatment for bulimia nervosa typically involves several therapy approaches. It is, however, complicated by several factors.

First, patients diagnosed with bulimia nervosa frequently have coexisting psychiatric disorders that typically include major depression (estimated to occur in 40%–70% of people with bulimia), dysthmic disorder [chronic mild depression], anxiety disorders, substance abuse disorders, or personality disorders. . . .

Although patients may have both bulimia nervosa and anorexia nervosa, a number of clinicians have noted that patients with predominate bulimia tend to develop impulsive and unstable personality disturbances, whereas patients with predominate anorexia tend to be more obsessional and perfectionistic. Estimates of the prevalence of personality disorders among patients with bulimia range between 2% and 50%. . . .

Treatment choices depend on the degree to which the bulimic behavior has resulted in physical damage and

Bulimia's main feature is eating an unreasonable amount of food in one sitting then purging by vomiting, taking laxatives or enemas, or abusing diuretics. (© **Kari Marttila**/Alamy)

whether the person is a danger to him or herself. Hospital inpatient care may be needed to correct severe electrolyte imbalances that result from repeated vomiting and laxative abuse. Electrolyte imbalances can result in heart irregularities and other potentially fatal complications. Most people with bulimia do not require hospitalization. The rate of hospitalization is much lower than that for people with anorexia nervosa because many bulimics maintain a normal weight.

Day treatment or partial hospitalization where the patient goes every day to an extensive treatment program provides structured mealtimes, nutrition education, intensive therapy, medical monitoring, and supervision. . . .

Outpatient treatment provides medical supervision, nutrition counseling, self-help strategies, and psychotherapy. Self-help groups receive mixed reviews from healthcare professionals who work with bulimics. Some groups offer constructive support in stopping the binge/purge cycle, while others tend to reinforce the behavior.

## Drugs, Psychotherapy, and Diet Counseling

Drug therapy helps many people with bulimia. Selective serotonin reuptake inhibitors (SSRIs) such as fluoxetine (Prozac) and sertraline (Zoloft) have been approved by the United States Food and Drug Administration (FDA) for treatment of bulimia. These medications increase serotonin levels in the brain and are thought to affect the body's sense of fullness. They are used whether or not the patient shows signs of depression. Drug treatment should always be supplemented with psychotherapy. . . .

Psychotherapy plays a major role [in] helping the individual with bulimia recover from the disorder. Several different types of psychotherapy are used depending on the individual's situation. Generally, the goal of psychotherapy is to help the individual change his or her behavior and develop a healthy attitude toward their body and food. . . .

A nutrition consultant or dietitian is part of the team needed to successfully treat bulimia. These professionals usually do a dietary review along with nutritional counseling so that the recovering bulimic can plan healthy meals and develop a healthy relationship with food. . . .

## The Prognosis Is Much Better with Treatment

The long-term outlook for recovery from bulimia is mixed. About half of all bulimics show improvement in controlling their behavior after short-term interpersonal or cognitive-behavioral therapy with nutritional counseling and drug therapy. However, after three years, only about one-third are still doing well. Relapses are common, and binge/purge episodes and bulimic behavior often comes and goes for many years. Stress seems to be a major trigger for relapse.

The sooner treatment is sought, the better the chances of recovery. Without professional intervention, recovery is unlikely. Untreated bulimia can lead to death directly from causes such as rupture of the stomach or esophagus. Associated problems such as substance abuse, depression, anxiety disorders, and poor impulse control also contribute to the death rate.

# The Physical Effects of Anorexia and Bulimia

## Pamela Carlton and Deborah Ashin

Pamela Carlton is a specialist in adolescent eating disorders and works as a physician in the Division of Adolescent Medicine at Stanford University School of Medicine. Deborah Ashin is a marketing consultant in the health-care and high-tech industries and a journalist who writes about parenting issues and technology.

Anorexia and bulimia can damage many different systems of the body. Most types of damage, such as loss of bone density, cognitive impairment, and heart damage result from the body's being deprived of essential nutrients. Other effects can be caused by purging—for example, self-induced vomiting can result in erosion of tooth enamel or tearing of the stomach or esophagus. Depending on the length and severity of the eating disorder, it may be possible to completely reverse most or all of the damage by restoring proper nutrition; however, in more severe cases permanent injury or death can result from anorexia or bulimia.

**SOURCE:** Pamela Carlton and Deborah Ashin, *Take Charge of Your Child's Eating Disorder: A Physician's Step-by-Step Guide to Defeating Anorexia and Bulimia,* Marlowe and Company, 2007, pp. 38–46. Copyright © 2007 by Marlowe and Company. All rights reserved. Reproduced by permission.

Eating disorders can have serious effects on every organ system in the body and, in some cases, may result in lifelong or even fatal consequences. . . .

Most of the medical complications described below are related to malnutrition, . . . defined as a state of improper nutrition, not just being underweight. Using this definition, a child can be of normal weight—or even overweight—and be malnourished if his proper nutritional balance is disturbed by not eating enough.

## Eating Disorders and the Heart and Circulatory System

The malnutrition caused by an eating disorder can seriously affect [a] child's cardiovascular system. As the heart becomes malnourished, it gets smaller, weaker, and less able to function at its normal strength, causing a range of problems: a slowed heart rate, decreased blood pressure, an irregular heartbeat, heart murmurs, heart attacks, and sudden death. Some behaviors that accompany eating disorders—such as vomiting or using medications to purge—may further damage the heart.

Signs of a heart problem may include fatigue, weakness, dizziness, passing out, poor circulation, and cold or blue extremities. People with eating disorders may not show any obvious physical symptoms, even though their hearts are severely weakened. In fact, they may still be engaging in normal activities, including rigorous exercise. Although heart problems seem to appear suddenly and without warning, they actually have been developing over a long period of time, because the body tries to protect the heart by using up all of its other reserves before depriving the heart of energy. Therefore, someone must be significantly malnourished before the heart is affected; and the heart must be significantly damaged before losing the ability to function normally.

Fortunately, the good news is most heart damage resulting from malnutrition or purging can be reversed when a patient returns to and maintains a normal nutritional state. . . .

## Hormones and Bone Density

Malnutrition, as well as purging, can turn down or turn off a part of the brain, called the hypothalamus, which controls the release of hormones throughout the body. When this occurs, the body will decrease the release of hormones such as estrogen, testosterone, and growth hormones, resulting in low sex hormones and low growth hormones. This can cause loss of menses, arrest of or failure to begin puberty, and delayed growth.

Adolescence is a critical time for skeletal development because . . . during this period, peak bone density is attained. Malnutrition from an eating disorder can cause the normal pattern of bone growth to reverse: instead of greater bone formation and less bone destruction, someone who is malnourished will have greater bone destruction and less formation. This puts them at risk for developing weakened bones (osteopenia or osteoporosis), which also increases the risk of broken bones.

A decrease in sex hormones (estrogen and testosterone) is the major reason why someone who is malnourished will have bone loss. The sex hormones affect the bones in two major ways: they inhibit bone destruction and they promote the absorption of calcium. If someone can't absorb calcium, his or her bones can't grow denser and, in fact, will decrease in strength and density. This is compounded by the fact that when someone is malnourished, he will not have adequate calcium in his diet. If there is not enough calcium present, and what is there can't be absorbed, bone loss—and osteoporosis—is very likely.

The duration and degree of malnutrition significantly influences the amount of bone loss a child may incur. Because children usually do not experience a significant loss of bone density in the first year of their eating disorder,

# How Anorexia and Bulimia Affect the Body

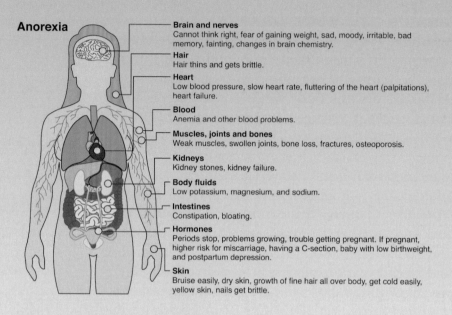

**Anorexia**

**Brain and nerves**
Cannot think right, fear of gaining weight, sad, moody, irritable, bad memory, fainting, changes in brain chemistry.

**Hair**
Hair thins and gets brittle.

**Heart**
Low blood pressure, slow heart rate, fluttering of the heart (palpitations), heart failure.

**Blood**
Anemia and other blood problems.

**Muscles, joints and bones**
Weak muscles, swollen joints, bone loss, fractures, osteoporosis.

**Kidneys**
Kidney stones, kidney failure.

**Body fluids**
Low potassium, magnesium, and sodium.

**Intestines**
Constipation, bloating.

**Hormones**
Periods stop, problems growing, trouble getting pregnant. If pregnant, higher risk for miscarriage, having a C-section, baby with low birthweight, and postpartum depression.

**Skin**
Bruise easily, dry skin, growth of fine hair all over body, get cold easily, yellow skin, nails get brittle.

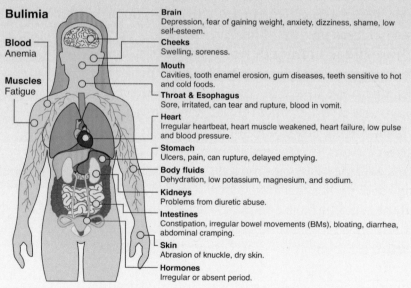

**Bulimia**

**Blood**
Anemia

**Muscles**
Fatigue

**Brain**
Depression, fear of gaining weight, anxiety, dizziness, shame, low self-esteem.

**Cheeks**
Swelling, soreness.

**Mouth**
Cavities, tooth enamel erosion, gum diseases, teeth sensitive to hot and cold foods.

**Throat & Esophagus**
Sore, irritated, can tear and rupture, blood in vomit.

**Heart**
Irregular heartbeat, heart muscle weakened, heart failure, low pulse and blood pressure.

**Stomach**
Ulcers, pain, can rupture, delayed emptying.

**Body fluids**
Dehydration, low potassium, magnesium, and sodium.

**Kidneys**
Problems from diuretic abuse.

**Intestines**
Constipation, irregular bowel movements (BMs), bloating, diarrhea, abdominal cramping.

**Skin**
Abrasion of knuckle, dry skin.

**Hormones**
Irregular or absent period.

Taken from: "Anorexia Nervosa Fact Sheet." The Office on Women's Health, June 15, 2009. http://womenshealth.gov /publications/our-publications/fact-sheet/anorexia-nervosa.cfm. "Bulimia Nervosa Fact Sheet," The Office on Women's Health, June 15, 2009. http://womenshealth.gov/publications/our-publications/fact-sheet/bulimia-nervosa.cfm.

early treatment is critical. Unfortunately, once bone loss occurs, it usually is not reversible. . . .

Children and adolescents who are malnourished may delay, or never reach, their expected adult height. In a malnourished body, the bones do not receive enough nutrition to grow longer because all of the body's energy is being used simply to stay alive. . . . Malnutrition may further stunt someone's growth by decreasing the production of growth hormone, which stimulates the bones to grow longer. . . .

## The Digestive System

The effects of malnutrition on the digestive system can be severe: the stomach can fail to deliver food properly to the intestines and the intestines themselves can fail to move food through properly. This overall slowing of the digestive system can result in many complications such as patients' feeling very full with minimal food intake, acid reflux, and severe constipation. A loss of the ability to sense hunger or fullness and the development of abdominal pain may also occur.

When people are malnourished, their liver can . . . develop . . . large fat deposits that may impair liver function. All of these effects on the digestive system are reversible with an extended period of proper nutrition.

Some people with eating disorders try to rid themselves of food (and calories) by purging, which can be in the form of self-induced vomiting, excessive exercise, or an excessive use of laxatives and/or diuretics. . . .

Repeated vomiting brings up harsh digestive acids into the esophagus and mouth, eroding the tooth enamel, gums, and the lining of the esophagus. With repeated forceful vomiting, it is possible to tear all the way through the esophagus or stomach. The hand or instrument used to induce vomiting can cut or tear the fragile lining of the mouth and throat; and the repeated pressure and acid from purging may also cause the esophagus or stomach to tear open, causing bleeding, which may be life-threatening.

The salivary glands may also be affected by purging. When these glands become overstimulated from vomiting, they can enlarge and form a mumpslike swelling in the cheeks.

Induced vomiting may also cause a loss of the natural "gag reflex"—the protective reflex, which keeps food, liquids, and vomit from entering the lungs. If foreign substances do enter the lungs, they can cause choking, severe difficulty breathing, pneumonia, and even death. The enlargement of the salivary glands and the loss of the gag reflex will probably reverse over time, but damage to the teeth, esophagus, and stomach may not.

Excessive laxative use may result in severe constipation and a reliance on artificial stimulation of the bowels in order to have a bowel movement. In extreme circumstances, the intestines may become so impacted with stool that they can rupture. Laxatives can also disrupt the balance of salts in the blood, sometimes to life-threatening levels. . . .

## Effects on the Brain

Despite the fact that many children and adolescents with eating disorders maintain good cognitive function well into their disease, in extreme cases, they may develop "organic brain syndrome." This is characterized by a "slowing" of brain function that causes significant cognitive difficulties. People with organic brain syndrome may display slowed thinking, in which they take longer to respond to questions than expected; forget what you told them right after you said it; and have difficulty with decision making. There are also psychological symptoms that occur when someone's brain is malnourished. These include extreme shifts in emotions, depression, anxiety, and obsessive-compulsive like symptoms. Rigid thoughts and rituals regarding food and meal preparation also frequently develop.

Imaging scans of brains of malnourished people show an actual decrease in the amount of brain tissue. Although we know malnutrition can change chemicals in the brain as well as blood flow to the brain, there is much controversy as to whether a malnourished brain will recover fully with proper nutrition. . . .

## Miscellaneous Impacts on the Body

Because malnutrition and purging can decrease the production of sex hormones (estrogen and testosterone), an eating disorder can stop sexual development, preventing puberty from starting or being completed. In girls, this can result in failure to begin menstruation or a loss of menstrual periods; boys may cease to have wet dreams or experience a loss of erectile function. Fortunately, there doesn't seem to be any effect on future fertility as long as the person has attained and maintained a healthy nutritional state.

The hematological (blood) system is also affected by malnutrition. All of the major types of blood cells—red blood cells, white blood cells, and platelets—may be affected. In most cases, once healthy nutrition is achieved, these conditions will be reversed. . . .

When someone is malnourished, the skin often becomes dry and flaky. Cuts and bruises don't readily heal and acne and rashes may develop. Because of a lack of body fat, a downy "fur" called lanugo may begin to grow on the body as an attempt to conserve heat and energy. People who purge may also develop calluses on their knuckles, where their knuckles hit their teeth. This is called Russell's Sign.

Malnutrition may cause someone's hair and nails to become dry and brittle. Their nails may develop pits and the hair on their head may thin and fall out. People with

> **FAST FACT**
>
> According to a 2009 study published in the *American Journal of Psychiatry*, anorexia has a mortality rate of 4 percent and bulimia 3.9 percent.

Signs of anorexia- or bulimia-caused heart problems may include fatigue, weakness, dizziness, passing out, poor circulation, and cold or bluish extremities. (© **Sally and Richard Greenfield/ Alamy**)

malnutrition do not usually develop bald spots, but their hair may become noticeably thin, dry, and brittle.

## Medical Complications of Improper Renourishment

Although . . . proper nutrition can halt or reverse many of the medical conditions created by an eating disorder, there are also very real dangers involved in how a child is "renourished." . . . Feeding a malnourished person too fast can have dangerous, life-threatening repercussions. It can result in a sudden drop of certain electrolytes (salts in the blood), causing problems with heart, lung, and muscle functions. Liver and kidney damage can also result. If not properly managed, refeeding can also cause a significant increase in fluid in the blood vessels, which may result in puffy hands, feet, and ankles, fluid in the lungs, heart failure, and even death. Therefore, it is extremely important to "refeed" severely malnourished people in a medically supervised environment.

# Current Research on Anorexia and Bulimia Will Lead to New Treatments

**Amy Novotney**

Amy Novotney is a staff writer for *Monitor on Psychology and grad-PSYCH*, publications of the American Psychological Association. She has a bachelor of science degree in journalism from Northwestern University.

In the following viewpoint Novotney discusses recent developments in research and treatment of anorexia and bulimia. She cites research indicating that anorexia and bulimia have a strong genetic component, helping to dispel the notion that people simply choose to have eating disorders. Other research has revealed brain abnormalities in bulimics, who have less activity in brain regions involved with impulse control. Other lines of research seek better treatment options. Cynthia Bulik, of the University of North Carolina, is testing the efficacy of online cognitive-behavioral therapy, which if successful would make it easier to treat hard-to-reach patients, such as those living in rural areas. Another recently developed approach teaches adolescent girls to critically examine cultural messages equating thinness with beauty, which resulted in a 60 percent lower rate of eating disorder onset.

**SOURCE:** Amy Novotney, "New Solutions," *Monitor on Psychology*, 40(4), April 2009. Retrieved from http://www.apa.org/monitor. No further reproduction or distribution is permitted without written permission from the American Psychological Association.

Only half of those with anorexia and bulimia recover fully, and even among those who have recovered from anorexia, many continue to maintain low body weights and experience depression, according to the Academy for Eating Disorders, a global professional organization dedicated to eating-disorders research, education, treatment and prevention.

To combat these numbers and encourage Americans to lead healthier lives, psychologists are leading battles on several fronts to eradicate eating disorders, help those diagnosed with or at risk for these disorders and debunk myths about these conditions.

## Genes at Work in Anorexia and Bulimia

Some of the most groundbreaking research is examining the genetic risk factors for eating disorders. Although for years experts believed anorexia and bulimia were caused solely by such environmental influences as peer pressure and societal expectations, recent work has shown that many genetic and biological risk factors are at play as well.

"It's not uncommon even in this day and age to see eating disorders referred to as 'choices by vain girls who just want to be skinny,'" says Michigan State University's Kelly Klump, PhD. "What we now know is that just like any other psychiatric condition, such as schizophrenia and bipolar disorder, eating disorders have a strong genetic component."

In her work examining the effects of genes on eating disorders, Klump conducted a series of developmental studies with data from the Minnesota Twin Family Study. She found that the heritability of eating disorder symptoms increases during puberty, from zero risk before puberty to 50 percent or greater after puberty. Along with Florida State University psychology professor Pamela Keel, PhD, Klump is now using those findings to examine how natural changes in ovarian hormone levels may contribute to bulimic behaviors in twins. Preliminary analyses suggest that heritability influences disordered eating most when estrogen levels are at their highest.

Klump is also involved with a study of the genetic underpinnings of anorexia conducted by University of North Carolina at Chapel Hill [UNC] psychologist Cynthia Bulik, PhD, and other researchers from around the world. As part of a 13-country Genetic Consortium for Anorexia Nervosa, they plan to conduct the largest ever genomewide association study for the disorder, pulling together resources and DNA samples of more than 4,000 females with anorexia and 4,000 controls.

"The name of the game in genetics is large samples . . . ," Bulik notes. "The hope is that the consortium will help us unlock the biology underlying the illness, an important step in developing biologically based interventions."

## Brain Differences in Bulimics

Meanwhile, new and as-yet-unpublished fMRI [functional magnetic resonance imaging] brain imaging work by Oregon Research Institute psychologist Eric Stice, PhD, suggests that in some females, bulimia may be hard-wired. Stice examined brain activation among 33 female adolescents and 43 young women after they tasted a chocolate milkshake. Over a one-year follow-up period, he found that those who showed greater activation of key reward regions in the brain—particularly the gustatory cortex, somatosensory cortex and striatum—reported increases in bulimic behavior.

"What I think we're learning is that if children are exposed to a high-fat, high-sugar diet early in development, they develop a strong preference for and craving for these foods that doesn't otherwise emerge, and that this is what sets people up for bulimia," he says.

Similar research by Columbia University's Rachel Marsh, PhD, shows that the brains of women with bulimia may react more impulsively than those without an eating disorder. Researchers compared fMRI images

from 20 women with bulimia to 20 similar-aged healthy controls while the participants identified the direction of a series of arrows viewed on a computer screen. They found that the women with bulimia tended to be more impulsive during the task, responding faster and making more mistakes than healthy women. They also found that the women with bulimia did not show as much activity in brain areas involved in self-regulation and impulse control. Marsh is now studying adolescents with bulimia to determine whether these functional brain abnormalities arise early in the course of the illness, possibly predicting its development and persistence.

A young Latina passes out anorexia and bulimia information. Researchers report that Latinos who have spent more than 70 percent of their lives in the United States have significantly higher rates of eating disorders than those who had spent more of their lives in their native countries.
(© AP Images/GDA via AP Images)

## Innovative Treatments

Psychologists are also at the forefront of several innovative treatments for eating disorders that target hard-to-reach populations, such as adult women and those in rural areas.

UNC's Bulik, in collaboration with researchers at the University of Pittsburgh Medical Center, is conducting a novel clinical trial to compare the efficacy and cost-effectiveness of an online cognitive behavioral therapy augmented with therapist-moderated, weekly online chat sessions with that of traditional face-to-face group therapy. The trial and follow-up will not be complete until [September 2013], but Bulik hopes the online program proves effective so it could help those in rural areas who suffer from the disorder.

Bulik is also partnering with fellow UNC clinical psychologist Donald H. Baucom, PhD, to test a couples-based anorexia treatment. Building on similar cognitive-behavioral couples' interventions for depression, anxiety disorders, smoking cessation and cancer, the program guides the healthy partner in how best to assist in recovery. . . .

Clinical psychologist Margo Maine, PhD, co-founder of Maine and Weinstein Specialty Group, based in Hartford, Conn., is also working with older adult women with eating disorders. Most of these women feel shame about their disorder, she says, thinking that they should have outgrown such "teenage" problems. Through individual therapy, Maine helps validate their experiences as women by discussing the many cultural and societal pressures women face in terms of perfectionism and weight and shape, and she encourages her clients to learn how to take time for themselves. . . .

## Evidence-Based Prevention

Other innovative work is seeking to thwart the development of eating disorders.

Stice, of the Oregon Research Institute, for example, developed an eating-disorder prevention program based on social psychology's theory of cognitive dissonance, in which participants critique the thin-ideal standard of female beauty through a series of verbal, written and behavioral group exercises. A 2008 *Journal of Consulting and Clinical Psychology* [*JCCP*] study with 481 adolescent girls who were dissatisfied with their bodies found that those who participated in the dissonance intervention showed a 60 percent reduction in eating disorder onset compared with controls who had no intervention.

Researchers are now testing the program's effectiveness when it's delivered by high school guidance counselors and physical education teachers.

"It all boils down to one simple premise— that if you take a critical analysis of [the thin ideal], you can talk yourself out of pursuing it," Stice says.

Adapting Stice's model, Trinity University psychology professor Carolyn Black Becker, PhD, has developed a peer-led eating-disorders prevention program that has significantly improved body-image perceptions and decreased disordered eating on college campuses. A study led by Becker also published in *JCCP* suggests that participants who attended two two-hour cognitive dissonance-based workshops showed less desire to be thin and were less dissatisfied with their bodies. This year [2009], the sorority Tri Delta and others will implement the program on 28 college campuses nationwide. . . .

> **FAST FACT**
>
> A pilot study conducted in Scotland in 2012 showed that anorexic and bulimic patients were more accepting of three-dimensional images of their bodies than traditional two-dimensional body images, suggesting that 3-D images could form the basis of new treatments.

## Disparities Continue

In spite of the growing research and innovative treatments, eating disorders are often undiagnosed, especially among ethnic minorities and men, researchers say. . . .

Bulimia and binge eating appear to be more prevalent among minority populations than once thought. In a series of articles in the November 2007 special issue of the *International Journal of Eating Disorders*, researchers reported that Latinos who spent more than 70 percent

# A Comprehensive Treatment Plan for the Eating Disorder Patient

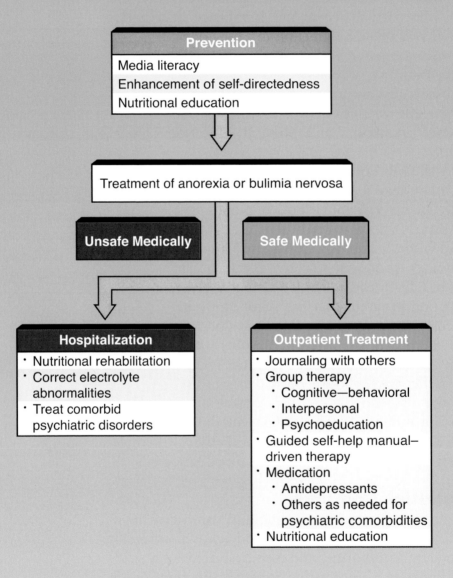

**Prevention**
- Media literacy
- Enhancement of self-directedness
- Nutritional education

↓

Treatment of anorexia or bulimia nervosa

**Unsafe Medically**        **Safe Medically**

**Hospitalization**
- Nutritional rehabilitation
- Correct electrolyte abnormalities
- Treat comorbid psychiatric disorders

**Outpatient Treatment**
- Journaling with others
- Group therapy
  - Cognitive—behavioral
  - Interpersonal
  - Psychoeducation
- Guided self-help manual–driven therapy
- Medication
  - Antidepressants
  - Others as needed for psychiatric comorbidities
- Nutritional education

Taken from: Kathleen N. Franco. "Eating Disorders." *Disease Management Project*, Cleveland Clinic, March 2012. www.clevelandclinicmeded.com.

of their lives in the United States had significantly higher rates of eating disorders than those who had spent more of their lives in their native countries. They also found that blacks who reported higher levels of acculturated stress were at greater risk for body image dissatisfaction and bulimia.

Overall, the study authors say, minorities often do not seek treatment for eating disorders, and they warn that the standard criteria for eating-disorder diagnoses may need to be revised for these populations. Latinos, for example, often exhibit binge-eating behavior rather than restricting their food intake and often will not appear skinny despite their irregular eating patterns, says Margarita Alegria, PhD, director of the Center for Multicultural Mental Health Research at Cambridge Health Alliance.

"We might just be asking the wrong questions," she says. . . .

All of these efforts may help save lives and lead to a healthier nation, says Kenyon College psychologist Michael Levine, PhD, an expert in eating-disorders prevention.

"Creating a world in which there will be fewer eating disorders will be one in which both men and women will be healthier because there won't be as much objectification and materialism, or as much emphasis on and preoccupation with thin and fat and control of appetite, shape and weight," Levine says. "I'm really excited about what the next 10 years hold."

# CHAPTER 2

# Controversies About
# Anorexia and Bulimia

# Cultural Messages Play a Major Role in Causing Anorexia and Bulimia

## Paul Campos

Paul Campos is a member of the law faculty at the University of Colorado at Boulder and the author of *The Obesity Myth: Why America's Obsession with Weight Is Hazardous to Your Health.*

In the following viewpoint Campos argues that pervasive cultural messages equating extreme thinness with female beauty play a strong role in the development of eating disorders such as anorexia and bulimia. Campos presents the example of Hollywood sex symbol Keira Knightley, who he notes has a body mass index (BMI) that puts her in the second percentile of the population (meaning that she is thinner than 98 percent of the population); he contrasts that with Brad Pitt, a male Hollywood sex symbol who has an average BMI. According to Campos, this unrealistic and distorted ideal of female beauty results in many women's developing deadly eating disorders such as the anorexia that killed one of his friends.

*Photo on facing page.* Runway models on the catwalk at a fashion presentation. Many researchers say that although Western society uses models to tout the ideal feminine form, most women are not built like models, thus creating a conflict for young women. (© Everett Collection, Inc./Alamy)

A friend of mine committed suicide earlier this month [February 2008]. That's one way of describing what happened.

Another way of describing the event would be to say she died from anorexia nervosa.

Yet another description would be to say she was killed by a culture that, from the time she was a little girl, tormented her constantly about her body.

Here's an e-mail a 14-year-old girl sent recently to Monique van den Berg, an English professor whose blog is dedicated to, among other things, encouraging people to stop hating their bodies:

> It's really hard not to judge yourself when the image of beauty is a size 0. I know I'm talented, but that doesn't make the girl in the mirror look any better. And every time my mom tells me I look pretty I just can't believe her! Is this just a '14-year old phase?' What'll it take for me to love my reflection? Because every time I say to myself 'You're beautiful' it feels like a lie.

## A Narrow Definition of Beauty

This girl has already learned two ignoble truths about appearance in our culture: That, as a woman, nothing she accomplishes will ever be considered as important as how she looks, and that the conventional definition of feminine beauty in our culture is both extraordinarily narrow and radically different from what most women look like.

Consider Hollywood's current It Girl, Keira Knightley. Knightley has a body mass that places her in the second percentile of the population. If her weight were to deviate as radically in the other direction—in other words if she were in the 98th percentile of body mass—she would weigh approximately 300 pounds.

Yet Knightley is presented by our media-industrial complex as a completely natural object of male desire,

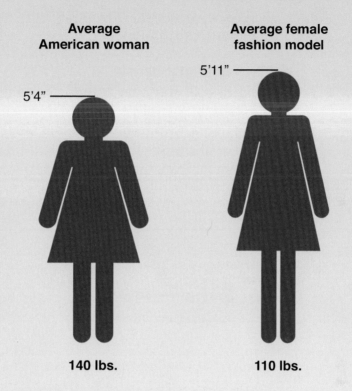

## Body Size of the Average Fashion Model Compared to That of the Average American Woman

**Average American woman**

5'4"

**Average female fashion model**

5'11"

140 lbs.

110 lbs.

Taken from: CNN, n.d. "Going to Extremes: Eating Disorders." www.cnn.com/interactive/2012/03/health/infographic .eating.disorders/index.html.

while men attracted to 300-pound women are considered to be in the grip of a bizarre fetish. (Meanwhile the archetypal male sex symbol Brad Pitt has a BMI [body mass index] of 27, which also happens to be the average BMI of middle-aged American men).

All this is reflected by a diet culture that tells girls and women to starve themselves, but not to the point where they actually have to be hospitalized (that would qualify as an "eating disorder").

As disturbing as so-called "pro-ana" [promoting anorexia] Web sites are (such sites offer cyberspaces where people with eating disorders reinforce each others' behavior, by, for example, posting photographs of their emaciated bodies as a form of what posters call "thinspiration"), I have a lot of sympathy for the adolescent girls who dominate these sites.

## Cultural Hypocrisy

These girls deal every day with the bottomless hypocrisy of a culture that screams at them that extreme thinness is synonymous with beauty, and that being fat, or rather "fat"—i.e., of average size—is a catastrophe, and then recoils in horror from the skeletal images—i.e., just slightly

American society puts too much importance on how a woman looks, says the author, plus the conventional definition of feminine beauty is radically different from what most women look like.
(© Chris Rout/Alamy)

thinner than Keira Knightley—those messages inevitably produce.

Those messages killed my friend, just as surely as they killed and are killing countless others (anorexia has the highest fatality rate of any mental illness, with perhaps half the deaths from the disease being suicides).

They nearly killed Diane Israel. Israel was an elite triathlete, who lost her career and almost her life to the all-too-common combination of disordered eating and compulsive exercise.

Israel has spent the last four years making a film called *Beauty Mark*, which uses her own experiences as a starting point to explore our culture's obsession with a narrow definition of beauty, and the self-destructive things people do to pursue it.

It's a powerful, important and often moving document (I appear in the film, but have no financial interest in the project). I wish my friend had lived to see it.

## FAST FACT

Following several high-profile deaths of anorexic models, such as Ana Carolina Reston in 2006, Spain and Italy banned the use of severely underweight models.

# Cultural Messages Do Not Play a Major Role in Causing Anorexia and Bulimia

## Sarah Ravin

Sarah Ravin has a PhD in clinical psychology from American University and is the professional adviser for Families Empowered and Supporting Treatment for Eating Disorders (FEAST).

In the following viewpoint Ravin argues that culture does not play a major role in the development of eating disorders. She discusses a well-known report on eating disorders known as the "Fiji study," which showed an increase in disordered eating in Fijian teenagers shortly after television was introduced to their society. According to Ravin, however, disordered eating (which she defines as "a persistent pattern of unhealthy or overly rigid eating behavior") is very different from actual eating disorders such as anorexia and bulimia. Ravin says that while most American women will exhibit disordered eating at some point in their lives, only a small percentage of women will develop anorexia or bulimia. Ravin claims that true eating disorders are caused by factors internal to the patient, such as neurobiology, personality traits, and genetics.

**SOURCE:** Sarah Ravin, "We'll Always Have Fiji," DrSarahRavin .com, October 16, 2010. Copyright © 2010 by Sarah Ravin. All rights reserved. Reproduced by permission.

I do not believe that the media plays a major role in the etiology [medical causes] of eating disorders. And yet, in much of the eating disorder world, it has become accepted as an unspoken, self-evident truth that patients with anorexia and bulimia have developed their illnesses in large part due to their desire to emulate "the thin ideal" which our media promotes. Those who espouse this idea cite the Fiji Study, which demonstrated dramatically increased rates of body dissatisfaction and disordered eating amongst Fijian adolescent girls within the first few years after television was first introduced to the island. . . .

As a feminist, I am a huge fan of [feminist social scientist Naomi] [Wolf's] work. In her groundbreaking book *The Beauty Myth*, she presents convincing arguments about the myriad ways in which our culture and society are toxic to women. I couldn't agree more.

## Disordered Eating and Eating Disorders

Our culture and society are harmful to all women and men, and certainly the media plays a huge role in triggering body dissatisfaction and disordered eating. (Incidentally, the media is a major culprit in the perpetuation of myths about eating disorders.) But disordered eating is not the same as an eating disorder. The Fiji study measured body dissatisfaction and disordered eating, not eating disorders.

The disordered eating/eating disorder distinction is not just a matter of semantics. In fact, I believe that eating disorders are quantitatively *and* qualitatively distinct from disordered eating, much as major depression is both quantitatively *and* qualitatively different from sadness. Anorexia nervosa has existed for centuries, long before the advent of television and internet and fashion magazines, and long before disordered eating became the norm.

I think it would benefit our profession tremendously to arrive at a consensus regarding the definition of "disordered eating" and how it differs from eating disorders.

## Anorexia and Bulimia Are Mental Illnesses

The confusion between eating disorders vs. disordered eating is a major contributor to society's (and some professionals') lack of understanding of eating disorders. People who engage in disordered eating are, on some level, responding to their environment in choosing to engage in certain eating behaviors, whereas people with eating disorders are caught in the grips of a terrifying mental illness which will not allow them to do otherwise.

Disordered eating is very widespread in our country, especially among women. I define disordered eating as a persistent pattern of unhealthy or overly rigid eating behavior—chronic dieting, yo-yo dieting, binge-restrict cycles, eliminating essential nutrients such as fat or carbohydrates, obsession with organic or "healthy" eating—coupled with a preoccupation with food, weight, or body shape.

By this definition, I think well over half of the women in America (and many men as well) are disordered eaters.

## FAST FACT

According to the famous "Fiji study," following the widespread introduction of television to the country, the percentage of subjects self-inducing vomiting to lose weight rose from 0 percent in 1995 to 11.3 percent in 1998.

## Anorexia and Bulimia Result from Internal Causes

The way I see it, disordered eating "comes from the outside" whereas eating disorders "come from the inside." What I mean is this: environment plays a huge role in the onset of disordered eating, such that the majority of people who live in our disordered culture (where thinness is overvalued, dieting is the norm, portion sizes are huge, etc) will develop some degree of disordered eating, regardless of their underlying biology or psychopathology.

In contrast, the development of an eating disorder is influenced very heavily by genetics, neurobiology, individual personality traits, and co-morbid disorders. Environment clearly plays a role in the development of eating disorders, but environment alone is not sufficient to cause them. The majority of American women will develop disordered eating at some point, but less than 1% will fall into anorexia nervosa and 3% into bulimia nervosa.

The Fiji study was indeed groundbreaking. It demonstrated the enormous impact of the media on teenage girls' feelings about their bodies and attitudes towards

In her book *The Beauty Myth,* author Naomi Wolf (pictured) presents convincing arguments about the many ways US society and culture are toxic to women. (© AP Images/ Jennifer Graylock)

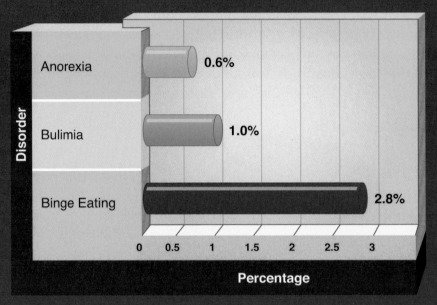

**Percent of the General Population with Eating Disorders**

Taken from: Nicholas Bakalar, "Survey Puts New Focus on Binge Eating as a Diagnosis," *New York Times*, February 13, 2007, p. F5.

food. But the study did not demonstrate a causal link between the media and eating disorders. Furthermore, our knowledge that the media makes girls dislike their bodies, while important in its own right, has not yielded useful information with regards to developing effective treatments for eating disorders. And isn't that the whole point?

I would like for our field [social science] to accept the Fiji study for what it is—a fascinating sociological study which confirmed empirically what we already knew intuitively—and push forward towards a deeper understanding of eating disorders so that we may develop and implement more effective treatments.

# Genetically Determined Tendencies Predispose Some People to Anorexia and Bulimia

## Tomas Chamorro-Premuzic

Tomas Chamorro-Premuzic is a professor of business psychology at University College London, an authority on psychometric testing and personality profiling, and author of several books, including *Personality and Individual Differences.*

In the following viewpoint Chamorro-Premuzic argues that genetic factors strongly influence the development of anorexia and bulimia. He cites a study of twins that showed a strong hereditary tendency to developing eating disorders and another study that found certain personality traits often associated with anorexia and bulimia. For example, those with perfectionistic and obsessional traits were much more likely to develop anorexia or bulimia. The author says that these genetically determined characteristics make some people much more susceptible to develop an eating disorder when exposed to stress, such as that produced by unrealistic portrayals of beauty in the media.

Most people think of eating disorders, such as bulimia and anorexia, as the result of contemporary beauty ideals fabricated by the media and the fashion industry. The underlying argument is quite simple: teenage girls (and increasingly boys) grow up admiring celebrities, which appear to come in smaller sizes every year. Thus there is growing pressure on young people to maintain a petit body structure; somewhat paradoxically, this pressure co-exists with unprecedentedly high rates of obesity in most Western societies. Are size-zero models really to blame for this? And why are we not getting thinner then?

Although over-eating and under-eating rates are both increasing, it is important to examine not only their social determinants, but also how these interact with personal factors. In the past five to seven years [he is writing in 2012], there have been robust psychological studies highlighting important genetic factors underlying the etiology [causes] of eating disorders. These factors also suggest that the degree to which the social context (including media-endorsed stereotypes) disrupts an individual's nutritional habits is by and large dependent on his or her personality.

## The Heritability of Anorexia and Bulimia

One of the most compelling sources of evidence for the heritability of eating disorders is a study published last year [2011] by Stephanie Zerwas and Cynthia Bulik. The authors review several decades of genetic research, including family, twin and adoption studies. Of these studies, the most powerful methodology for disentangling the effects of nature and nurture is no doubt twin designs. Given that identical twins are twice as similar to each other in their genetic makeup as non-identical or fraternal twins are, a comparison of eating disorders rates between identical and non-identical twins should enable us to estimate the degree to which nature (shared genes) in-

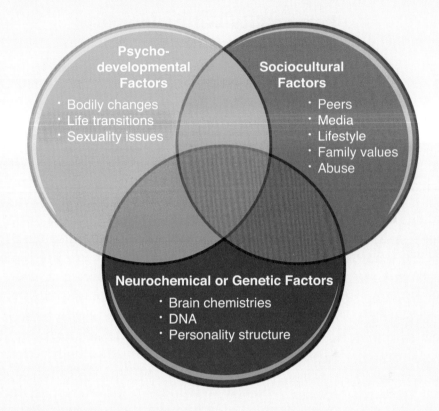

## Genetic/Biological Factors Interact with Other Variables to Cause Eating Disorders

**Psycho-developmental Factors**
- Bodily changes
- Life transitions
- Sexuality issues

**Sociocultural Factors**
- Peers
- Media
- Lifestyle
- Family values
- Abuse

**Neurochemical or Genetic Factors**
- Brain chemistries
- DNA
- Personality structure

Taken from: A. Natenshon. *When Your Child Has an Eating Disorder: A Step-by-Step Workbook.* Carlsbad, CA: Gürze, 1999.
Image found at: www.s126869113.onlinehome.us/10.html.

fluences eating disorders. The authors found that, among white Caucasians, eating disorders have a substantial hereditary basis. For example, in a study conducted with a US-representative sample of Minnesota twins, [Kelly] Klump reports [in 2009] that 50 percent of the variability of individual differences in eating disorders can be attributed to genes. That said, until puberty, genes contribute 0 percent risk, which means that a potential vulnerability towards eating disorders is only "activated" when individuals reach puberty (no doubt because of biological changes as well as changes in environments and interests, such as sexual relationships).

## Personality Determinants of Anorexia Bulimia

In a widely cited study (published in 2005), Stephanie Cassin and Kristin von Ranson reviewed a decade of research into the personality determinants of anorexia, bulimia, and binge eating. Their findings suggest that personality plays a role in each of these pathologies, and that the same set of traits is frequently associated with different types of eating disorders. For example, anorexia and bulimia are much more common in perfectionistic and obsessional individuals, who also tend to have low emotional stability (or low EQ [emotional quotient]). However, anorexia is more common in individuals with high constraint and low novelty seeking, whereas bulimia is more common in individuals with high impulsivity, high sensation seeking, and high novelty seeking (all of which are typical of more open and creative individuals). An interesting finding of this study was that self-report inventories are often inaccurate to investigate the causes of eating disorders because individuals with the above personality characteristics often misreport and misinterpret their symptoms.

Although the above studies indicate that eating disorders are influenced by biological factors linked to people's personality, these effects are probabilistic rather than deterministic. What this means is that personality increases a person's predisposition to suffer from eating disorders: whether s/he does or not will depend on how this vulnerability interacts with environmental factors. What are these environmental factors? Anything that is experienced by the person as stress, and here is where the

> **FAST FACT**
>
> According to the Academy for Eating Disorders (AED), anorexia and bulimia have a comparable degree of heritability to other psychiatric disorders, such as bipolar disorder and schizophrenia.

People with perfectionist or obsessive traits, like frequent hand washing, are much more likely to develop anorexia or bulimia. (© John Greim/ Science Source/Photo Researchers, Inc.)

media probably plays a role in shaping people's dietary habits. If you have the wrong personality profile, you will be much more likely to interpret stereotypical media beauty ideals as presssure to be thin, so the media will act as stressor. But the effects that these media messages will have on individuals will depend on their personality. Moreover, personality affects people's self-perceived body mage, and how satisfied they are with their bodies. Unsurprisingly, some of the same traits that predispose people to eating disorders are responsible for people's distorted body image representations.

# Websites That Promote Anorexia and Bulima Are Harmful and Should Be Censored

## Rebekah McAlinden

Rebekah McAlinden is a nineteen-year-old recovering from anorexia and bulimia. She is currently a student at Mary Andrews College in Sydney, Australia.

In the following viewpoint McAlinden argues that "thinspiration" websites that promote anorexia and bulimia are very harmful to those who are suffering from eating disorders and that such websites should not be allowed to exist. She relates that they were personally harmful to her when she was suffering from anorexia and bulimia and that it helped her recover when her support network discovered she was visiting such sites and prevented her from accessing them. Having largely overcome her eating disorder, she wishes to raise awareness about the harm these sites do. She suggests that what young people access on the Internet needs to be monitored, and websites that promote disordered eating should be blocked.

Three years ago [in 2009], if you had logged onto my computer and looked at my recent history, you would have discovered I frequently trawled through pro-eating disordered websites. There are communities of males and females of varying ages on sites such as *Live Journal, Tumblr, Facebook* and *MySpace* all promoting anorexia as a lifestyle choice, rather than a mental illness.

These websites, filled with "thinspiration" tips and tricks to achieve weight loss, fuelled both my Anorexia and Bulimia and significantly harmed my health. Many of the eating disorder sufferers only support weight loss for others, to receive the same support in return.

After struggling with my body image for years and engaging in eating disordered behaviours, I now eat regularly, do not over-exercise, do not manipulate my diet in any way, do not binge and purge and do not abuse laxatives. I am still in recovery from my eating disorder, but have come a long way in the last six months.

## Thinspiration Websites Should Not Exist

Doing some research on common misconceptions about eating disorders for my recovery-focused blog *R is for Recovery* (and Rebekah), I stumbled across a webpage called [site name removed]. The website claims not to be a "pro-ana" [promoting anorexia] site, but rather a "pro-skinny site." Basically the site host uploads pictures of very normal and average sized celebrities and models, labels them as fat and uses insulting and crude language to articulate their hurtful (and in my opinion, downright wrong) opinions.

The site also has a "Starving Tip of the Day." This website is not unique—there are a number of similar pages on the internet condoning eating disordered behaviour—websites that individuals frequently visit. They are harmful to everyone—not just young women or young men; not just those in recovery from eating disorders; not just parents or teenagers or children—but harmful to all those who are at risk of believing such lies about their bodies and then engaging in eating disordered behaviour.

So, after I contacted Melinda [Tankard Reist, author and advocate for women and girls] about my concerns around these sites, she posed this question: "How, as a young woman in recovery, do these sites make you feel?" Outraged! I am so angry that these sites exist and that young adults are buying into the lie that being thin should be a high priority. The fact that we disrespect our bodies; the fact that we struggle to comprehend all bodies are different and the fact that we manipulate food to love ourselves more—does it not all seem a little wrong to you?

As a young woman in recovery, seeing others succumb to such behaviours is triggering, distressing and saddening. Why do these websites that encourage restricted diets and treating our bodies in such an awful manner exist? The point is that they shouldn't. The point is that we need to monitor what our young people are exposed to on the internet. The point is that we should be in favour of healthy bodies, healthy minds, healthy lifestyles—none of which are reflected in an eating disordered lifestyle.

> **FAST FACT**
>
> Researchers at the University of Cincinnati describe pro–eating disorder sites as "Online Negative Enabling Support Groups (ONESG)," a new kind of social support network that reinforces harmful behaviors in participants.

## Blocking Harmful Websites

I am blessed to have a wonderful support network—it has been one of the biggest and most useful things for me throughout my recovery. Having people I can be accountable to and be honest with about what was (and occasionally still is) going on in my eating disordered mind has saved me from so much. Once these friends were aware of my frequent visits to eating disordered sites and my eating disordered Facebook account, that was the end of that! Internet sites were blocked, Facebook passwords were changed and I learnt to break some of the bad habits I had been indulging in.

I also attended an outpatient program at RPAH [Royal Prince Alfred Hospital] in Sydney, and a day program associated with the hospital. Seeking medical treatment is a must for all eating disordered patients. The day program in particular helped me to normalise my eating patterns and realise I was responsible for my own choices, I could not possibly live the rest of my life entrenched in the eating disorder and I really needed to, as well as deserved to, change and deal with what was going on in my life. And so I've done that. Also, as I began to eat regularly and feed my brain and body again, I started to think more clearly—it's definitely part of the process of ridding oneself of the 'ED [eating disorder] voice' once and for all.

So my aim today is to create awareness of these sites so that we can take action against them. If you are a parent, please, please monitor your child's internet history.

Websites that promote "thinspiration" contribute to the anxiety that anorexics and bulimics feel about their condition. (© NetPhotos/Alamy)

If you are in recovery from an eating disorder and struggle to avoid opening these types of websites, let someone know. Perhaps ask a friend to block them for you. If you're courageous enough, block them yourself. If you are a friend or sibling to someone who has struggled with body image and eating disordered behaviour, ask them how they're doing—regularly check in with them and allow them to be accountable to you.

If we can all support each other in this endeavor and choose to steer clear of pro-anorexic and bulimic sites, perhaps it will be one small but significant change to reducing the prevalence of eating disorders—and the terrible harm and suffering they cause.

# Websites That Promote Anorexia and Bulimia Should Not Be Censored

## Mary Elizabeth Williams

Mary Elizabeth Williams is a staff writer for the online magazine *Salon*, a radio commentator, and author of the social commentary book *Gimme Shelter*.

In the following viewpoint Williams argues that attempts to block "thinspiration" websites that promote anorexia and bulimia, while well intentioned, will not work. According to the author, attempts at censorship simply motivate the pro–eating disorder community to develop work-arounds or find new places to post their content. A better solution, Williams suggests, is to set up a system where searches for thinspiration content prominently return links to organizations such as the National Eating Disorders Association, so that those seeking pro–anorexia/bulimia content will be exposed to more healthful resources. She points out that this is already being successfully done in other areas—for example, when someone googles "suicide," the first result they see is for the National Suicide Prevention Lifeline.

SOURCE: Mary Elizabeth Williams, "Pinterest's Anorexia Dilemma," *Salon*, April 17, 2012. www.salon.com. Copyright © 2012 by Salon. All rights reserved. Reproduced by permission.

It's a lesson that keeps getting learned on the Internet: You can't make bad things go away with a flick of the delete key. So when, last month [March 2012], instant memo generator *Tumblr* and beloved cat lady destination *Pinterest* updated their terms of service to discourage pro–eating disorder sentiment, they did not, in fact, actually cure eating disorders.

The attempt to tamp down the shadowy pro–eating disorder community has been raging nearly as long as the community itself has existed. It's a well-intentioned effort. But every new opportunity for social media is also a new opportunity for like-minded spirits to converge in anonymity. You don't have to look far online to see the vibrantly sad and scary pro-ana (as in anorexia), pro-mia (as in bulimia) worlds alive and well and starving themselves to death.

## Censorship Is Not Working

So despite the ostensible crackdown, you can still find plenty of #thinspo [thinspiration] on *Pinterest*, with photos of whippet-skinny women and encouragement not to stop "until you're proud" and "see a 0 on your clothing tag." Likewise, you can find plenty of #thinspo reminders on *Tumblr* that "Empty stomach, you'll learn to love it . . . ." And a quick search for "thinspo" on *Instagram* turns up well over 46,000 tagged photos, with haunting streams from "just another anamia insta" (that's anorexia/bulimia Instagrammer) and another user who declares she "needs to be skinnier." There are gaunt images of jutting collar- and hipbones, as well as devastating tableaux like a photo of a Coke and candy with the caption "I'm such a mistake and I'm not strong. I hate me," or a user's screenshot from a calorie-counting diary app that declares, "If every day were like today, you'd weigh 76.8 lbs in 5 weeks."

> ### FAST FACT
>
> A study published in *Pediatrics* in 2006 found that 96 percent of visitors to pro–eating disorder websites and 46.4 percent of those visiting pro-recovery sites, learned new techniques for purging or losing weight.

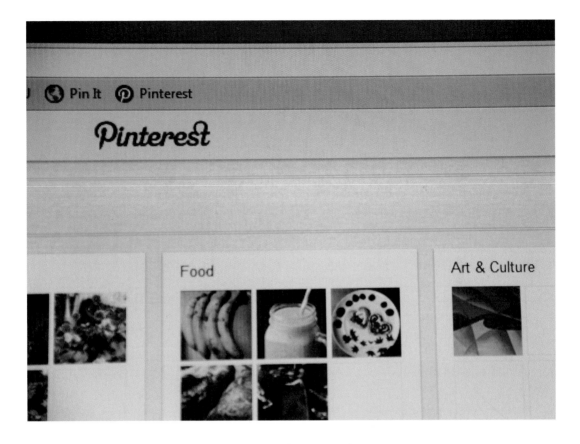

The more things change, the more they stay the same. Sites like *Instagram, Tumblr* and *Pinterest* are now grappling with the same issues that *Facebook* and *Twitter* and, back in the day, regular old blogs have for years. And unfortunately, they're finding the challenge just as awkward and often ineffectual as their predecessors.

The hope that sites have a moral obligation to their users to create an environment that is safe and healthy and nontoxic doesn't always jibe with the practical reality of making it happen—not when the demand for "thinspiration" is so persistent, and the cultural obsession with weight so pervasive. We see it in the way that a single tweet from Miley Cyrus about not eating a Carl's Jr. and Lady Gaga hashtagging #PopSingersDontEat turn into major news stories and rumors of anorexia.

The website Pinterest recently updated its terms of service to discourage users from promoting eating disorders. (© Linda Jones/Alamy)

# Message in a Website

A 2006 review of pro-anorexia websites found they pushed ideas of perfection, isolation, control, and deceit, among others.

## Prevalent Themes Extracted from the Pro-Ana Websites

| Theme | Description |
|---|---|
| Control | Websites alleged that successful weight loss helps control a person's body and life. |
| Success | Success was associated with strength and measured by weight loss. Only those who are strong can lose weight successfully and keep the weight off. |
| Perfection | Society and cultural "norms" equate thinness with perfection and support its pursuit. |
| Isolation | People with eating disorders are alone. Befriending the eating disorder leads to isolation from others. |
| Sacrifice | Foregoing friends, school, family, and relationships is necessary to foster continued success with the eating disorder. The websites encourage this sacrifice. |
| Transformation | Eating disorders can transform a person from being "fat and ugly" to being "thin and beautiful." The transformation is fostered by successful and continued weight loss. |
| Coping | Eating disorders are a means of coping with difficult life situations (abuse, troubled relationships, death) and problematic feelings (sadness, loneliness). The websites offer a way to cope or manage the eating disorder as opposed to "treating" the eating disorder. |
| Deceit | Individuals may have to deceive others to protect their eating disorder. Hiding weight loss and abnormal eating attitudes and behaviors is necessary to prevent discovery of the eating disorder. |
| Solidarity | These websites allow people with eating disorders to survive in a world that views the eating disorders community as tragic, dangerous, and disgraceful. The websites are a place where the eating disorder community can remain strong and supportive of one another. |
| Revolution | Individuals with anorexia nervosa should channel their strengths in other areas of life that require reform. |

Taken from: Mark L. Norris. et al., "Ana and the Internet: A Review of Pro-Anorexia Websites," *International Journal of Eating Disorders*, vol. 39, no. 6, September 2006, p. 446.

## A Better Solution

It's the right of any site to determine its content—or at least try to. But as Denise Restauri in *Forbes* points out, all that happens when you merely set up roadblocks is that a community gets clever about finding work-arounds and starts "house hunting" for new places of refuge. To really effect change, what communities need are dedicated and sensitive leaders who can work with members—talk to them and point them to healthy resources. And they need to create tools that cannot just flag content but respond to it. Note, for example, what happens when you Google "suicide." Your first result is for the National Suicide Prevention Lifeline, and the query "Need help?" Organizations like the National Eating Disorders Association need not only to be present on sites like *Pinterest* and *Instagram*, they need to show up right away when users are creating #proana or #thinspiration content.

The tragic truth is that a person who posts her self-loathing over drinking a Coke is not going to be helped by simply being blocked or forced to choose a more vague hashtag. Halfhearted attempts to cut her off from a community that cheers self-destruction aren't enough. She needs more than rules to make her stop posting. She needs guidance out of the darkness. She needs real people who can help her stop hurting herself.

# Men with Anorexia or Bulimia Face Special Challenges

**Fredy Tlatenchi**

Fredy Tlatenchi is a senior reporter for the *Daily Sundial,* the student newspaper and website for California State University–Northridge (CSUN).

In the following viewpoint Tlatenchi claims that men who suffer from anorexia and bulimia face unique stigma and isolation. The author says that media portrayals depict the typical victims of eating disorders as privileged blonde girls, rendering male sufferers invisible. He notes that the American Psychological Association says one in four anorexics are male, but in a survey of CSUN students with eating disorders, only 10 percent were men. Tlatenchi admires women with the strength to speak out publicly about their struggles with eating disorders, and he challenges men to embody their own strength by doing the same. According to Tlatenchi, men with anorexia and bulimia need male role models and need to know they are not alone.

**SOURCE:** Fredy Tlatenchi, "Men Should Speak Up About Anorexia," *Daily Sundial,* February 27, 2012. Copyright © 2012 by Daily Sundial. All rights reserved. Reproduced by permission.

On a good day you will find me carefully dressed, eating a hamburger and reading an ebook on my iPad between classes.

You cannot tell from my demeanor that I suffered from anorexia nervosa for six years.

Take a cue from television shows and you would be led to believe that only women developed anorexia nervosa, bulimia nervosa or a binge eating disorder. Willowy blonde girls with far too much money and friends,

Men who suffer from bulimia or anorexia face stigma and isolation and need role models to know they are not alone, says the author. (© Angela Hampton Picture Library/ Alamy)

who live in Pleasantville, USA are the usual victims, while male characters seem to be secure about their body image, if nothing else.

## Suffering in Silence

But I know that isn't true. Six years of my life were spent proving that stereotype wrong.

From early high school to my junior year at CSUN [California State University–Northridge] I hid my disorder under a pile of baggy clothes and low self-esteem, motivated to remain at 115 pounds despite standing at 5'11. Coupled with my disorder were an obsessive fear of being fat and the need to test myself against the hunger pains shooting through my stomach.

Anorexia nervosa, as defined by the National Eating Disorder Association, is characterized by a refusal to maintain body weight or be above a normal weight. Fearing becoming fat, anorexics have a distorted body image that cannot be cured with dramatic weight loss.

I have never met another male who was willing to admit that they suffer or had suffered from an eating disorder, but I know there are more of us out there.

According to the American Psychiatric Association, one male suffers from anorexia nervosa for every four females who do. In a survey of 3000 CSUN students, out of 28 percent of individuals who reported having an eating disorder, only 10 percent were male.

Dr. Veronica Stotts, a staff psychologist at CSUN, said women are more likely to develop eating disorders by sampling certain behaviors from their friends, whereas men are less likely to share these behaviors among friends.

## FAST FACT

In 2008–2009 males composed 10 percent of hospitalizations for eating disorders, up from 6.5 percent a decade earlier.

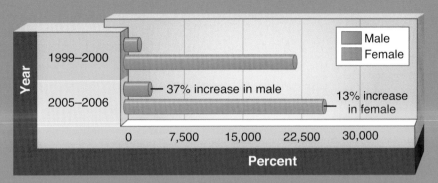

**Male and Female Eating Disorder Hospitalizations in the United States**

37% increase in male

13% increase in female

Year: 1999–2000, 2005–2006

Percent: 0, 7,500, 15,000, 22,500, 30,000

Male / Female

These data were taken from AHRQ, Center for Delivery, Organization, and Markets, Healthcare Cost and Utilization Project, Nationwide Inpatient Sample, 1999, 2000, 2005, and 2006.

Taken from: Renee Park and Marita Vera, "The Downside of Eating Too Healthy: Orthorexia Nervosa," Medill Reports, n.d. http://news.medill.northwestern.edu/chicago/news.aspx?id=150389.

## The Need for Male Role Models

Stotts currently coordinates JADE, Joint Advocates on Disordered Eating, a peer counseling group that promotes awareness and prevention of eating disorders among college students. In a group of 12 people, I am its only male member.

There is a stigma attached to being a recovered "starvin' Marvin"—as a former friend once put it—or being a male with any other eating disorder.

Eating habits become an issue to your family and friends, and well-intended stereotypes on television suddenly become as offensive as racial slurs being shouted into your ear. One is viewed as damaged or fragile, not realizing the amount of fight one needs to recover; after all, one is fighting one's self.

I so admire the young girls and women strong enough to come forward about their history with an eating disorder or [who] want to raise awareness and prevention.

Yet, despite all the bravado and testosterone society wants from its men and perpetuates in its media, so few come forward when this issue is discussed. Even less are willing to help those in need.

I never had a male role model guide me through those six years and I wish I had. I simply wanted to hear a phrase that ultimately would help both women and men in that situation: "You're not an anomaly."

# Anorexia and Bulimia Are Increasingly Affecting Older Women

### Trisha Gura

Trisha Gura is a molecular biologist with a PhD from Northwestern University. She is the author of *Lying in Weight: The Hidden Epidemic of Eating Disorders in Adult Women* and contributed to *Going Hungry: Writers on Desire, Self-Denial, and Overcoming Anorexia* and *Body: The Complete Human.*

In the following viewpoint Gura argues that eating disorders are far from being just a teenage problem; older women are increasingly affected by anorexia and bulimia. She notes that recent statistics show that three times as many women in their forties and four times as many women in their fifties are entering treatment for eating disorders now compared with in the mid-1990s. According to the author, older women are feeling more cultural pressure to look thinner and are experiencing major life transitions that have been shown to trigger eating disorders in susceptible individuals. Gura calls for more effort to understand and prevent eating disorders among older women.

They do it even in their 90s.

Adult women starve, binge, and purge. Eating disorders, once thought to be the province of misguided teens who twist the cultural thinness imperative into ravaged bodies, are now rampant in the aging, health-conscious, baby boomer population. And beyond.

That's the news, according to a recent Associated Press (AP) article. In fact, the situation has been brewing for some time and is only now gaining national attention. Women in their 40s and 50s are showing up for treatment in numbers triple and quadruple those of ten years ago. (The greatest surge has occurred in the last 5 years.) The influx is so great that some treatment centers are creating special programs for older patients. One step further, the Park Nicollet Health Services' Eating Disorders Institute near Minneapolis, MN, is building a new facility . . . that will offer a special treatment track for mature patients.

How old is "mature?"

How about 92? That was the age of the oldest woman in my book, *Lying in Weight*. She was originally hospitalized for pneumonia and, as she recovered, ate prunes and walked laps around the hospital ward. She felt horrible about lying around and getting fat.

## Distorted Thinking

Other women I interviewed for *Lying in Weight* were also living proof that the old saw, "You can never be too old to be thin," holds true.

Take Nilda, who at 68 was diagnosed with anorexia for the first time.

"Why?" I asked her.

"Because I'm running out of time, and I need to get my affairs in order," she replied.

What she meant is that she was afraid to die and leave her children bereft. Ironically, she was killing herself, subsisting on black coffee and toast. But distorted thinking is a hallmark of anorexia; Nilda's fears about dying were so strong that they wouldn't allow her to eat, which can only hasten the inevitable.

Nilda's story further reinforces the idea that eating disorders are about issues happening to "mature" women, in addition to teens striving to look like skeletal fashion models. Eating disorders happen to individuals who have a certain temperament ("genetic predisposition") and use destructive food behaviors and/or overexercise to cope with major transitions that occur throughout the lifespan. Genes load the gun. Environment pulls the trigger.

## Misguided Coping Strategies

Consider Janet, who was 56 when I interviewed her. She was caught in the midst of a perfect midlife storm: an empty nest, divorce, and menopause. And fears about "looking too old" as she went online trying to find a new partner. She turned to bulimia to cope.

Janet's "coping" routine illustrates the horrors of an eating disorder in an adult woman. At 5'7" and 95 pounds, Janet regularly diets, vomits, and purges through overexercise. She eats half a bagel for breakfast, a tiny salad for lunch, and strawberries or an artichoke, along with a bottle of wine, for dinner. The stomach acid churned up from routine vomiting eroded her teeth—which have all been replaced. When she's not skimping on caloric intake through dieting and purging, she's using maniacal workouts to exorcise what few calories do get burned—every day she follows up her minimum five-mile run with a spinning or aerobics class at her gym.

The circumstances behind Janet's tragic story are becoming all too common; according to my research, adults face 15 major transitions during their lifetime, each with

> **FAST FACT**
>
> Women aged sixty-five to eighty are equally likely to feel concerned about their body shape or to "feel fat" as are young adult women, according to researchers at Oregon Health & Science University.

the capability of triggering a new eating disorder or reviving an old one. The transitions, which range from marriage and divorce to retirement and late-life realities, don't necessarily cause the eating disorder. Rather, eating disorders result from a mix of genetics, cultural, and psychological factors, some of which start very early in life and seed a latent problem. And then, another stressor emerges, launching the eating disorder into full gear.

## Stressful Life Transitions

So which transitions are the most stressful and most likely to trigger a new or latent eating disorder? Answer: all of them. Here are just a few examples:

- *Marriage*. Jo acquired anorexia for the first time after she married a minister, relocated to a new parish, and tried to be the "perfect wife." Partners add to the complexity because they bring their own attitudes and baggage to a relationship in which the eating disorder drives them apart as a couple.
- *Pregnancy*. Tracy, with a history of bulimia, got excited when pregnant because morning sickness gave her an easy way to "not get too fat." Other women—if they can conceive—actually cut back or stop the eating-disordered symptoms during pregnancy because they experience the time as permission to be fat and a chance to do for someone else, their growing fetus, what they cannot do for themselves: eat. Maternal instincts often trump psychopathology.
- *Parenting*. Lauren relapsed into bulimia after the birth of her daughter. With a wave of her car keys, she would tell her husband that she was going out to the grocery store. There, she would buy a bag of junk food, eat it in her car and throw up behind a dumpster. Other mothers who are suffering with their own food issues experience conflict with a toddler at mealtimes, a school age child refusing food

or vomiting after overeating, or an adolescent acquiring an eating disorder in a recreation of her mothers' nightmare.

No, this is not just teen stuff. And as baby boomers age and feel the cultural pressure to look younger (read "thinner") the transitions associated with eating disorders will only become all the more potent.

## Prevention and Support

How do we curb the rising numbers of people in need of help? To be sure, opening more specialized treatment centers that target mature audiences is a good thing. But that's the back end of the equation; we also need to learn how to anticipate the triggers beforehand and set up support systems for women who are going under. We need to help people discover ways of coping other than through self-destructive and self-defeating measures. Physicians,

Older women are becoming increasingly affected by anorexia and bulimia. Recent studies show that since the mid-1990s three times as many women in their forties, and four times as many in their fifties, have sought treatment for eating disorders. (© **Bubbles Photolibrary/ Alamy**)

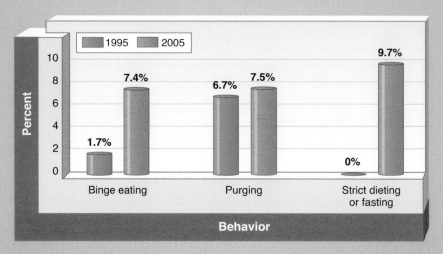

## Eating Disorder Behaviors in Australian Adults Age 55–64 in 1995 and 2005

- 1995
- 2005

Percent

Binge eating: 1.7% (1995), 7.4% (2005)
Purging: 6.7% (1995), 7.5% (2005)
Strict dieting or fasting: 0% (1995), 9.7% (2005)

Behavior

Taken from: Phillipa J. Hay et al., "Eating Disorder Behaviors Are Increasing: Findings from Two Sequential Community Surveys in South Australia," PLoS ONE, February 6, 2008. www.plosone.org/article/info:doi/10.1371/journal.pone.0001541.

therapists, counselors, and social workers need to tune their radar screens to eating disorders, especially those on the front lines such as gynecologists, fertility experts, and dentists (they're often the first to see the signs of bulimia—eroded teeth, as in Janet's case).

This is a wake-up call for prevention. We need to deconstruct eating disorders in older women, before they become realities that affect whole families and create legacies passed down to children.

As a society, we need to make it possible for family and friends to be comfortable about discussing eating disorders. Healing might even involve marital counseling or family therapy in which the mother is the patient. Even though eating disorders are sometimes visible, as in cases of anorexia or binge eating disorder, they are usually closet issues. One woman I interviewed had bulimia for 35 years and her husband never knew. Ironically, he was a detective.

The stakes are high and growing. As medical science pushes the frontiers on longevity and people now fast to extend their lives, imagine the catastrophe, the costs to our health care system and to families who suffer loving their wives, mothers, and grandmothers, who do it when they're 100.

# Anorexic or Bulimic Patients Who Refuse Treatment Present Ethical Dilemmas

## Maureen Kelley and Douglas J. Opel

Maureen Kelley is a practicing psychologist in New Jersey who works with children, adolescents, and families. Douglas J. Opel is an assistant professor in the Divisions of Bioethics and General Pediatrics at the University of Washington School of Medicine.

In the following viewpoint the authors present a case study of an anorexic woman named Pam who will not accept her diagnosis or agree to treatment. The case raises ethical concerns about the capacity of patients with serious eating disorders to make decisions about their treatment and the appropriateness of imposing involuntary treatment. Opel says that the two possible ethical approaches are to either err on the side of protecting the patient or respecting their autonomy, and he points out that in a case such as this, the choices are mutually exclusive: Fully respecting her autonomy means not fully protecting her, and vice versa. Kelley argues that to treat the patient against her will risks undermining the trust and cooperation that are essential to recovery and suggests an approach of compassionate support and ongoing negotiation with the patient.

SOURCE: Maureen Kelley and Douglas J. Opel, "Denial," *The Hastings Center Report,* vol. 40, no. 6, November/December 2010, p. 11.

Pam is an eighteen-year-old with a history of depression. She has been hospitalized for the past six months for severe weight loss and dehydration. When admitted, she was diagnosed with acute inflammation of the pancreas and gallbladder, but it became clear that these issues were secondary to a diagnosis of anorexia nervosa. Her weight upon admission was seventy-six pounds. Pam refuses to accept this diagnosis and will not cooperate with any provider who refers to "anorexia" or attempts to discuss her eating disorder.

As a pragmatic strategy for providing care, the medical team has largely avoided referring to anorexia or eating disorders when treating her. But Pam is not the only problem. Pam's mother, the only family member directly involved in her care, also refuses to acknowledge her daughter's anorexia and has supported Pam's extremely restrictive requests to control her hospital meals as she regains her ability to eat by mouth. Prior to admission, Pam was living at home with her mother. She has no contact with her father.

Now that Pam's acute condition has improved, the medical team worries that any further complicity in her denial of her anorexia will hinder attempts to begin eating disorder treatment protocols. Consultants from adolescent medicine and psychiatry tried having a frank discussion with Pam and her mother about Pam's underlying eating disorder. This conversation only succeeded in making them both angry. Her mother ultimately threatened to "fire" these physicians.

The medical team and hospital decide to pursue involuntary commitment to treat Pam's anorexia if she does not agree to treatment. Yet when a consulting surgeon recommends that Pam's gallbladder be removed, Pam is allowed to consent to surgery. Soon thereafter she is evaluated by a mental health professional, who decides that Pam does not meet criteria for involuntary commitment. Pam insists she be discharged.

Her primary nurse couldn't help but wonder: does Pam have the capacity to make medical decisions, or doesn't she?

## Commentary by Douglas J. Opel

The distorted body image and unrealistic perceptions that give rise to denial in anorexia pose an interesting ethical issue: how does this distortion and denial affect the patient's capacity to make treatment decisions? It could be argued that Pam's refusal to acknowledge her disorder represents a lack of the insight and comprehension required to make decisions about treatment. This, in turn, could call into question her decisional capacity and provide justification for involuntary commitment. The clinicians in Pam's case seem to be making this claim. But their other actions—such as obtaining Pam's consent to remove her gallbladder—seem to imply the opposite. How can we declare that a person both retains and lacks decisional capacity at the same time?

The answer to this question might simply be that assessments of capacity should be specific to the decision in question, rather than a global assessment. Therefore, even though we might think Pam lacks capacity to make decisions about her feeding regimen, we may still consider it appropriate to respect her autonomy in other decisions, such as whether to remove her gallbladder. But herein lies the rub: where does anorexia begin and end? Can treatment decisions in this case really be separated into "anorexia-specific" and "other"?

## Two Ethical Approaches

When it is difficult to discern which decisions are adversely affected by the patient's underlying disease, there are two possible ethical approaches: (1) err on the side of respecting autonomy and allow the patient to make some decisions that perhaps she does not have the capacity to make, or (2) err on the side of protecting the patient by

Anorexic and bulimic patients who refuse treatment for disorders that may kill them present an ethical dilemma to medical professionals. (© Daily Mail/Rex/Alamy)

narrowing the scope of decision-making authority, thus failing to fully respect the patient's autonomy. Option one has practical appeal in this case because of the need to engage the patient in her recovery with a disease that is centrally about control. However, option two seems to have equal appeal for anorexia and other mental illnesses because of the difficulty in determining the effect the disease has on any decision.

Even though the standard model of decision-making capacity is not a global assessment and option one is likely the path most people would prefer, I think Pam's case should make us pause. First, given Pam's lack of capacity to make feeding decisions, I think there are situations where her reasons for agreeing to a cholecystectomy [surgical removal of the gallbladder] matter. For example, if the surgeon's recommendation is merely that her gallbladder can be removed, but that doing so is not essential, then her reasons for wanting the surgery are important—for instance, what if she wanted her gallbladder out because getting rid of an organ would allow her to lose more weight? (Of course, if there are clear medical indications for the cholecystectomy, Pam's reasons for consenting would not matter.) Second, it seems artificial to put decisional boundaries on a disorder like anorexia. While there is a spectrum of how pervasive the distorted thinking in anorexia is, it certainly can be so pervasive that it penetrates one's identity. In these situations, any attempt to determine an "anorexia-specific" treatment decision is meaningless. Although Pam's case may not be this severe, the psychological component of her disease seems to be significant enough that its global effect on her decision-making should be considered.

Pam's case highlights the difficulty in distinguishing her anorexia from her other medical issues and consequently, the difficulty her clinicians face in trying to protect her from harm while respecting her autonomy. Pam challenges us to rethink our approach to determining capacity in mental illness. Perhaps we should err on the side of patient protection by narrowing the scope of decision-making authority.

## Commentary by Maureen Kelley

The psychological features that many anorexic patients show—clinical depression, delusions, a distorted body image, and the need for control—can hamper their capacity to make safe choices about their health, limiting their ability to give informed consent. A patient's fixation on being thin often supersedes all other values, including survival. While harmful preferences are often honored in adult patients out of respect for autonomy—respecting a patient's freedom to make choices, albeit not necessarily good ones—when teens and adults express suicidal ideation, more paternalistic interventions are usually viewed as ethically warranted to prevent immediate harm to self. Patients suffering from self-inflicted, chronic starvation are slowly killing themselves, yet the bar for involuntary commitment remains fairly high, as reflected by the refusal to commit Pam to a rehabilitation program. So why was this not done to keep her safe?

**FAST FACT**

Some people with eating disorders exhibit anosognosia, a condition in which they are unable to recognize or take seriously their mental illness.

The explanation for this seeming ethical inconsistency is partly pragmatic and partly rooted in an appeal to long-term consequences. Caring for young adults with anorexia can be challenging and heartbreaking for medical teams and families alike. While short-term, involuntary treatment may be necessary if a patient's medical situation is critical, evidence shows that the best chance for long-term recovery in a rehabilitation program occurs when patients come to voluntarily accept treatment. Supportive family members and a trusting relationship with care providers are essential to this process. Yet control and denial are central features of this illness, and Pam's mother is complicit in her denial. Given these facts, how do you save Pam from herself?

Patients like Pam are often smart, driven achievers. Despite their illness, they are capable of functioning well, of hiding harmful behavior, and of manipulating parents, family, and the care team. Pam's attempt to dictate the hospital menu, deny her diagnosis of anorexia, and fire hospital staff illustrate her desire for control. Because she refuses to address her underlying illness, the team can do

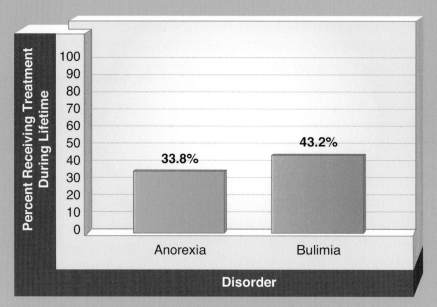

**Lifetime Treatment Rates for Anorexia and Bulimia**

Percent Receiving Treatment During Lifetime

Anorexia: 33.8%
Bulimia: 43.2%

Disorder

Taken from: National Institute of Mental Health. www.nimh.nih.gov/statistics/1EAT_ADULT_ANX.shtml; www.nimh.nih.gov/statistics/1EAT_ADULT_RBUL.shtml.

little more than respond to the acute symptoms of that illness. Yet by playing along with the charade, Pam's mother and the care team are complicit in Pam's denial, preventing her from taking the first step in facing her disease. For this reason, the team should insist on honesty as a necessary part of a successful care plan. Presenting a united front could possibly defuse the threat of being fired.

## Trust and Cooperation Are Essential to Recovery

Not unlike long-term treatment for substance abuse or serious depression, long-term recovery from anorexia requires a cooperative, committed patient. For anorexic patients, relinquishing control over weight and food can short-circuit this process. When treating a disease that is centrally about psychological control, a strategy of "tough love" that takes decision-making rights away risks undermining what trust exists between the team and the patient and losing the patient to follow-up.

Hope for patients like Pam will likely be found in a strategy of compassionate but honest support, persistence, and creative but firm negotiation from the medical team and family—for example, making enrollment in an outpatient eating disorder program a condition of discharge. Unfortunately, the ideal of shared decision-making between patient, physician, and family is predicated on honesty about the diagnosis and supportive family members who will back the medical team. If Pam's mother can't appreciate the gravity of her daughter's situation, perhaps another family member—her father, grandmother, aunt, or even a close friend—could help Pam face her illness, so that over time, she can find healthy alternatives to harmful self-deprivation.

Even with family support, however, the road to recovery often involves medical crises and multiple admissions. Clinical teams may face the difficult decision to discharge a patient who is slowly starving herself and wait for her to get sick and scared enough to voluntarily enter a treatment program. The hope is that by working toward a support network that values honesty rather than reinforces denial, patients like Pam, when confronted with a choice about treatment, will be more likely to find the strength to make healthy decisions.

# CHAPTER 3

# Personal Experiences with Anorexia and Bulimia

# Developing Anorexia as a Response to Grief

### Ian Sockett, as told to Linda Harrison

After he lost his beloved grandmother, Ian Sockett began to starve himself. As he relates to journalist Linda Harrison in the following selection, he thought that the physical pain that resulted from restricting his food while maintaining a strenuous exercise regimen was easier to deal with than the emotional pain he felt. Soon the anorexia began to take a toll on his life—he lost his friends, was unable to attract a girlfriend, and his family was continuously worried about him. When his declining health resulted in a serious chest infection requiring hospitalization, Sockett says he experienced a wake-up call. He decided to turn his life around and fulfill his childhood ambition of running a marathon. Although his return to health and fitness was an arduous journey, he persevered and is now happy to have a second chance at life.

*Photo on facing page.*
Saving a teen from the ravages of an eating disorder often requires professional and family help. (© **BSIP SA/Alamy**)

**SOURCE:** Ian Sockett, as told to Linda Harrison, "'I Began to Starve Myself. . . .'" *The Independent,* July 19, 2011, p. 18. Copyright © 2011 by the Independent Print, Ltd. All rights reserved. Reproduced by permission.

As I lay in my hospital bed, I'd never felt so scared or alone. I glanced at my painfully thin body, emaciated by 25 years of anorexia. At 5ft 7in, I weighed five stone [70 pounds]. After years of surviving mainly on coffee and fruit salad, while continuing to push myself to exercise almost every day, my body couldn't take any more.

I had pneumonia, a collapsed right lung and was in urgent need of a blood transfusion. I was also in isolation so, although I desperately wanted to see my parents, I couldn't. The seriousness of my situation hit me for the first time. I knew I might die in this room, alone.

To explain how I found myself in this dark place, I need to go back 25 years, to a very different time. I was 15, a top-grade student tipped to be the next head boy who represented the school and county in athletics, rugby and cricket—I was the Midlands 400m [meter] champion. Life was great. My parents and teachers had high hopes.

## Bottled-Up Grief

Then my beloved grandmother, or Nana as I knew her, died of an aneurysm. I'd been very close to Nana—my brother Andrew and I used to stay with her and Granddad when my parents were at work. While Granddad was quite a strict disciplinarian, Nana was softer and spoilt us. Losing her was my first experience of death, and of losing anyone close. I was devastated but I was also confused. I couldn't accept that the rest of the world was continuing as though nothing had happened. Didn't anyone realise my Nana had died? I felt my life had come to a grinding halt.

I don't know why I didn't talk about my feelings. But I kept thinking that maybe this was what it was like for everyone, and how could I burden my mother with this when she'd just lost her mother?

I realise my reaction to the situation was peculiar, but maybe not as uncommon as you might think. I rationalised that if I was physically hurting, this would somehow make the pain of losing Nana easier to deal with. I could not justify being happy and carrying on as if nothing had happened.

So, quite simply, I began to starve myself. Slowly at first, but maintaining the same level of sporting activity. My body started to hurt when I ran but I was determined, no one was going to stop me. And so the pattern began. Once you start to starve yourself you find you can manage to exist on smaller and smaller amounts. You soon learn the calorific content of everything.

My running was one of the first things to suffer. I no longer had the energy to perform at the same level. This made me angry but I couldn't stop, even though I had a constant gnawing pain in my gut. I couldn't accept that I wasn't as good as I used to be and this made me angrier and more miserable.

## Self-Induced Isolation

By the time I took my A levels [standardized tests in Britain], I was on the hamster wheel of self-punishment, driving myself harder while existing on fewer and fewer calories. I was no fun and didn't want to go out, so inevitably friends stopped asking me. Soon, there were no friends.

Studying gave me the perfect excuse to shut myself away in my room, too busy to eat at mealtimes. I was amazed when a tutor suggested I apply to Oxford—I was just Ian Sockett from the local secondary school in rural Herefordshire. I passed the entrance exam and went for the interview, but I didn't want to go to university, by now my life had imploded. I didn't get accepted and when the rejection letter arrived it confirmed what I already knew—I was no good.

I got a local job in sales and marketing but my parents were extremely worried about me. Eating disorders are difficult for the sufferer but perhaps even more so for family and friends, who can't understand why someone won't eat. I eventually agreed to seek professional help, but back then the thinking around anorexia, especially in men, was hardly advanced.

The experience felt horrific. I was referred to what most people would call a psychologist, who asked if my parents had sexually abused me. I was disgusted. He was talking about the only two people who hadn't given up on me, who'd cried rivers of tears watching their son disappear before their eyes. I left feeling sickened. I did not go back.

By 2007, I was holding down a professional job with the local authority [government], and working 11-hour days at M&S [Marks & Spencer, a department store] at weekends. This seven-day routine had been going on for almost three years, and was another form of self-punishment—why should I let myself enjoy my weekends? I weighed less than six stone [84 pounds], I always felt cold, rarely laughed and was a truly frightening sight.

By now I'd got used to people staring, even though it hurt. I heard people whispering, they assumed I had cancer or AIDS. None of those applied to me. The reason I didn't have a girlfriend was simple—I looked hideous.

For men, things are exacerbated because admitting to having an eating disorder isn't macho. People think it only affects teenage girls responding to messages from the fashion industry. This isn't true. I knew exactly how I looked; there was no body image deception. I hated what I saw and detested having my photo taken. Anorexia was a way of self-harm, of punishing myself.

## A Wake-Up Call

My wake-up call came the following year. I caught a chest infection and when two courses of antibiotics failed, I was admitted to hospital. I began 2008 being told I had pneumonia and my right lung had collapsed. The doctors kept me in as they wanted to "hit me hard" with intravenous antibiotics to try to control the infection.

During my first afternoon, the hospital closed to visitors to contain an outbreak of norovirus, or the winter vomiting bug. Hours later, due to taking antibiotics, I got the runs. I was placed in isolation over fears I had contracted the virus. I found myself alone, stuck within four walls and banned from seeing anyone. I felt weak and soon became very, very afraid. My mum was outside, left to imagine what was happening.

I was so frightened that it suddenly dawned on me just how precious life really was. I realised I might never leave the hospital. Despite feeling very weak, alone and terrified, I'd already made my decision. I was going to get out of this dreadful situation and do something to repay society for all those wasted years. It may sound strange, but I started to formulate my goal. I'd fulfill my childhood ambition of running a marathon. I'd make my parents proud of me again. I knew it wouldn't be easy, but those same traits of bloody-mindedness and determination would help me win the greatest battle of my life.

> **FAST FACT**
>
> Eating disorders can be triggered by an absence of support after a life trauma such as physical or emotional abuse or the death of a loved one, according to a 2012 report in the *Journal of Clinical Nursing*.

I decided to run for Macmillan Cancer Support. I'd started fundraising for them while at M&S and one thing that had stayed with me was how Macmillan was there for everyone affected, not just the individual but family and even friends. Sometimes we just need someone to give us a hug, hold our hand or to be close. Lying alone in hospital, I empathised with how important that was.

The journey back to health and marathon fitness was long, frustrating and difficult. You don't change a 25-year way of thinking overnight. You're in a routine, you think, "what's going to happen if I change that and do something different?" But I started eating three meals a day, and the sky didn't cave in and nobody died. This enabled me to keep going. I also needed to put on weight slowly—too fast could have caused my heart to overload and internal organs to fail.

## Getting a Second Chance at Life

There were plenty more tears. I kept thinking, "I'm never going to make it." But I knew I couldn't let anyone down. My greatest motivator was the thought of completing a marathon, hanging that medal around mum's neck and saying, "Thanks for being there." I'd also been accepted to run for Macmillan, and I owed them a debt of gratitude for believing in me. Plus, it no longer hurt to run, I could really put some power behind it. Food became fuel for me. I didn't want any therapy or professional support. Besides, very little was available in my area.

My first marathon was Paris 2009. The residing memories are the pain in my quads [front thigh muscles] during the last few miles and the words "Go, Soko, go" yelled by one of the Macmillan support team, balanced precariously up a French lamp post.

I did it, I completed my first marathon. And I've not stopped since. I'm 41 and I do some form of exercise every day, either running, swimming or going to the gym, and I weigh about nine stone [126 pounds]. I've raised more than 10,000 [pounds Sterling] for Macmillan.

I've run the London Marathon twice, each year beating my previous time. I completed this year's [2011's] in three hours, 13 minutes and 55 seconds, which gave me automatic qualification for 2012.

Of course, I wish I could turn back the clock 25 years and start again. But while I might have wasted those years, I've been given a second chance and I don't intend to waste one minute of it. . . .

For me, having a reason, or several reasons, to recover from anorexia was pivotal. What's important to remember is that no matter how deep a hole you've dug yourself into, there's always a way out. I'm living proof.

# An African American Woman Recovers from Anorexia and Bulimia Through Faith and Family Support

### Ashley Michelle Williams

Ashley Michelle Williams is a broadcast and digital journalist who works at NBC network news. In the following viewpoint she shares her story of growing up as an African American woman dealing with depression, prejudice, and racism. She believes such issues, as well as trying to fit into mainstream images of beauty that were not appropriate for her ethnicity, triggered her anorexia and bulimia. The effects on her body when she purged frightened her, but it was only when her family found out about her behaviors that she decided to seek help. Through counseling, family support, and her religious faith she was finally able to recover from her eating disorders.

S ecrets can truly bind us—and sadly even kill us—if we allow them [to]. I decided to let go of my secret, and I've realized that sharing it with the world could help others.

In this society, most people want to believe that African-Americans and minorities in general do not have eating disorders. From an early age, I knew that many women struggled with eating disorders. Yet as a young African-American woman, I never thought it would affect me. I was wrong. Not only did I suffer from one eating disorder, I suffered from two.

I started dieting when I was around 12-years-old, often starving myself just to fit in with my peers who were Caucasian and had a very different body type from me. I kept comparing myself with them, and although I had amazing, loving parents and family members who told me I was beautiful and encouraged me to love myself, that still didn't stop me. I battled anorexia, then bulimia.

## FAST FACT

In an online survey conducted by Dr. J. Renae Norton, 12.6 percent of eating disorder patients reported symptoms of bulimia, 20.9 percent reported symptoms of anorexia, and 48.2 percent reported a combination of anorexic or bulimic symptoms.

I think I tried to stop for a moment. I just wanted to be normal. I tried hard to do this on my own without seeking help. But still that feeling that I was *too fat* kept coming to me. I craved food, but I didn't want to get fat. So instead I heard about bulimia and thought it would be better. I convinced myself that I was still technically ok, because I "was eating."

The way I felt after purging would scare me. Sometimes my heart would have irregular beats, sometimes my esophagus would hurt very much, and sometimes I felt like the blood would rush to my head. The anxiety of hiding all of this was overwhelming, and suffering through it knowing what I was doing to my body was terrifying.

## Racism and Depression

I finally knew that I had to stop once my sister caught me. She ran to my parents and told them, and they were so scared and worried about me. They started to really console me and talk with me. I decided to seek help for my eating disorder from [a] psychologist.

Although it was hard to stop, I was able to do so by looking deep within myself at the real reasons why I was doing this. Dealing with racism and depression from other issues in my childhood, I realized that those had prompted me to not love myself and who I was. I think that prejudice and racism can be huge triggers in sparking eating disorders and depression for many minorities, because we have often long[ed] to be very similar with groups of people who are not of our ethnicity. Many times we crave to fit into the mainstream.

I didn't realize this at first, but looking back, I think this could have triggered my eating disorder. I often compared my body to theirs. Addressing these issues with people I loved and a psychologist helped me to heal and to really begin to love myself just the way I was. I realize that regardless of your ethnicity, we all have different body shapes and we all are beautiful just the way God made us. There is nothing wrong with being different. In fact, it is being different that people often want to be and make people become aware of new things.

Writing this, and sharing my secret with the world is hard, but I truly believe that God did not allow me to go through these issues and to heal from them if I was not meant to use my experience to help make a difference in someone else's life. I hope that each of you who are reading this now will have the strength be inspired to either seek help if needed or to encourage someone you know to seek help.

## A Leap of Faith

As a young journalist now, I am driven to share untold stories with the world on teen issues. The stories I have done that have granted me the opportunity to research eating disorders have awakened me to how stereotypes can kill, how we can kill each other, and how we need to help one another through these problems.

I believe that I went through this at such a young age to use my story to uplift others and to encourage others, especially African-American women, to never allow society's perceptions of you to hold you back from getting help.

My advice to anyone who is suffering is to take that leap of faith. Gain the courage to reach out and talk to someone about what you are going through. You don't want to wait until it's too late. You don't want to not live the life that you wished to one day have. Therefore, go to one of your school's counselors and set up times to meet with them. This is what I did in my recovery. I started talking with a counselor at my high school. . . .

Yet, most of all, my last piece of advice is to be honest with your loved ones and your family. Being honest with the people around you will unlock your battles and help you to get the treatment that you need. It hurt me that my sister caught me throwing up, but in a way, I am glad. I am glad that my family was so willing to help me overcome these disorders and to finally just live my life without having a regretful feeling every time I wanted to eat food.

My message to the world—especially African-Americans—to embrace and love yourself just as you are and to never be ashamed to seek help. This test . . . This battle that you are going through will one day help someone else as I hope my story will also encourage you.

Remember, we are all beautiful and we each have something powerful to offer to the world. You just have to believe it. God never makes mistakes and He loves you more than you will ever know. He wants to use you and your experiences to help others begin to help themselves. Never lose faith and always know that there is a rainbow through the rain.

# A Childhood Ruined by Her Mother's Anorexia

**Sian Selby**

In the following viewpoint Sian Selby describes what it was like grow-ing up with an anorexic mother. She says her mother had volatile mood swings and strange controlling behaviors around food. For example, her mother might give her extremely specific shopping instructions and go into a rage if she brought home the wrong thing (such as tuna in oil instead of in water). According to Selby, her mother was unable to admit that she had an eating disorder, even when she ended up in the hospital with chest pains. When her moth-er died from her disease at age forty-eight, Selby went into therapy to deal with her anger at not having a normal childhood.

My mother had so many different personas. On one hand, she was funny, wacky and a talent-ed artist who never gave herself credit for the outstanding drawings she created. But then she was also volatile, stubborn and an expert liar. Mum was so good at manipulating me and pretending there was nothing wrong with her. She never once admitted the fact that she was anorexic—even though she'd been battling it since she was 16.

I wish I'd known that my mum's mood swings, controlling tendencies and weird food habits were all part of her illness, then I wouldn't have been so angry with her all those years. I didn't know exactly why, I just knew our situation wasn't normal.

My parents split up not long after I was born. Dad was an alcoholic. I'd see him on weekends and he'd take me to McDonald's and give me money to spend on food. Sometimes he'd take me supermarket shopping; I'd bring all the groceries home, but Mum would often go mad and throw most of it out. I became good at hiding stuff in my room and eating it in secret. I was also lucky that my mum's parents lived only a few minutes up the road, so I'd have dinner at their house at least once a week. They were the most stable relationship I had at that time; they were my saviours. However, I never said to them, 'Things aren't right at home, I need your help'. The food was enough for me—I didn't want to upset Mum.

> ## FAST FACT
>
> In a study published in the *Journal of Personality Disorders* in 2000, 61.8 percent of anorexic or bulimic patients also suffered from a personality disorder, most commonly avoidant personality disorder or borderline personality disorder.

## Unpredictable Mood Swings

Mum always said we had to eat healthily, yet she gave me vegetables from a can, never anything fresh. When I had friends over, she'd serve tinned [canned] spaghetti. If she made me a packed lunch, it might be a lettuce sandwich with no butter—just bits of bread and a piece of lettuce.

Some days, I'd come home from school and Mum would be really nice and relaxed. She'd sit next to me and draw while I'd do my homework. Other times, she'd fly off the handle about the slightest thing. Mum would send me to the shops with very specific instructions. I once came home with a tin of tuna in oil instead of brine and she went ballistic and told me to go back and exchange it. I had some pocket money so I bought a tin of tuna in brine for her and secretly ate the tuna in oil.

If Mum was happy and having a good day, she'd want to cuddle me, but it was more upsetting than comforting because she was just skin and bones. She always felt cold. Her hands were often freezing and, even on warm days, she would wear baggy jumpers [sweaters].

It would've been easy for me to fall into the trap of adopting my mother's attitude to food.

I was lucky that I had friends and family around me encouraging my passion for food and pointing out that I was too skinny because I wasn't eating a lot.

Mum and I had some massive fights when I was a teenager and I moved out when I was 18.

## In Denial Until the End

She'd always show up at the bank where I worked and it got really bad. Three years later, I decided I had to make a fresh start, so I got a transfer and moved an hour and a half away. One of my aunties organised a big family party for my 21st birthday at a restaurant. I'd written a really nice speech thanking my mum, but she didn't turn up. When we were leaving, we saw her outside. She said she'd been too sad to come in because I was 21 and was growing up. I was so upset that I just walked away. Mum always made everything about her.

A month later, I got a call from another aunt, who had taken Mum to the hospital because of chest pains. When I arrived, Mum looked so ill. She'd deteriorated so much, but she wouldn't let the doctors do any tests. She kept insisting that she was fine. I told her, 'If you don't get help, the next time I see you, you'll be in a box'. She didn't react, and checked herself out of hospital. That was the last time I saw her alive. My mother passed away three weeks later. It was October 2008 and she was only 48 years old.

I wish I could've shown her the death certificate and said, 'See, this is proof. It's written down. You had anorexia and it killed you'.

I saw a therapist after Mum died and all this anger came out. I was angry that I didn't get a proper childhood.

I was angry that she never got any help. After I finished therapy, I just felt sad. Sad for her that there's this whole other life that she missed out on and sad that she can't be here to see me. Once your mum is gone, it leaves this big empty space that nothing can ever fill.

# Saving a Teenage Daughter from Anorexia

## Harriet Brown

Harriet Brown is the author of *Brave Girl Eating: A Family's Struggle with Anorexia*. She also edited *Feed Me: Writers Dish About Food, Eating, Weight, and Body Image*. In the following selection Brown shares the story of how she saved her daughter Kitty from life-threatening anorexia. She describes the early, puzzling signs that something was wrong with Kitty, the gradual realization that her daughter was gravely ill with anorexia—a realization brought home by a medical emergency—and how she and her husband nursed their daughter back to health using the intensive family-based therapy known as the Maudsley Approach.

I t was Kitty's 14-year check-up in February 2005 when I first became worried about her weight. She'd always been on the small side, but she'd grown an inch and put on some muscle after joining a gymnastics team, yet she weighed less than she did the year before.

SOURCE: Harriet Brown, "How I Saved My Daughter's Life: A Mother's Story of Anorexia," *The Telegraph*, February 26, 2011. Copyright © 2011 by the Telegraph. All rights reserved. Reproduced by permission.

Four months later, on a family outing, she cried continuously and told me that she couldn't stop worrying. 'Worrying about what?' I asked. She shook her head, her eyes hidden from me, and said no more.

Most parents of an anorexic child can look back on a day when they should have done something but didn't. A day when they first realised something was very wrong but still had no words for it, just a feeling.

For me it was the next day, the Monday after Mother's Day, when Kitty rang me at work to ask what we were having for dinner on Friday night—five days later. I wish, now, that I'd paid attention to the frantic tone in her voice, to the anxiety driving this odd and insistent questioning.

Over the next month Kitty's mood continued to deteriorate. She cried more; she was testy one moment, clingy the next. . . .

## A Sudden Passion for Cooking—but Not Eating

In her chipper moments she couldn't stop talking about her new passion for cooking. She spent hours reading cookbooks, marking pages with yellow Post-its, making lists of ingredients—lobster, Cornish game hens, cream, tarragon, butter. . . .

The thing was, she didn't actually eat what she cooked. A bite here, a nibble there, that's all. She always had a reason: this dish upset her stomach, she wasn't in the mood. Jamie, my husband, and Emma, Kitty's 10-year-old sister, and I ate what she cooked, and it was delicious. But Kitty's behaviour left a bitter aftertaste.

I started watching her. Watching what she ate, and didn't eat. Watching the way goose bumps ran up her arms on a sunny afternoon. How her head suddenly looked too big for her body.

At her end-of-year graduation in early June Kitty wore an orange halter dress she'd borrowed from a neighbour.

From across the crowded gymnasium I saw my daughter with different eyes, away from the usual context of our lives, and what I saw made my heart begin to pound. In an auditorium crowded with 14-year-olds she was by far the thinnest girl in the room.

The next morning I booked the first appointment I could get with Dr Beth, Kitty's paediatrician. I knew what was going on now. I couldn't help it. I saw that Kitty was starving herself. I just didn't know what to do about it.

I cooked her favourite foods and watched in frustration as she pushed them away, or took two bites and insisted she was full. Once upon a time family dinners had been a ritual I looked forward to, a time when we came together to talk and laugh. Now I dreaded them.

. . .

## A Medical Emergency

A few weeks later Kitty wakes me up one night to tell me that her heart feels 'funny'. There is fear in her deep brown eyes, different from the anxiety I've been seeing since this nightmare started. I know this is serious.

On the way to accident and emergency Kitty sits next to me in the front seat, her lank blonde hair scraped back in a ponytail, looking small and lost in the oversized sweatshirt that fitted her six months ago. 'I'm dizzy, Mummy,' she murmurs.

I keep one hand on the wheel, the other on her, as if I can keep her from floating away. My brain seems to divide as I drive, so that while part of me is watching the road, hitting the accelerator and brake, another part is thinking, 'Don't die. Please don't die.'

When we arrive her heart rate is dangerously low and she is taken to the intensive care unit. The doctor tells me he wants to use a feeding tube, but Kitty becomes so distressed that I ask for an hour more; he agrees on the condition that Kitty must eat some food.

## Eating as an Act of Courage

The nurse brings a chocolate protein milk-shake and a straw. She helps Kitty sit up, Kitty reaches for the milk-shake, holds it in one hand, lifts the straw to her lips. Tears slip over the sharp cliffs of her cheekbones. Her whole body trembles. For five minutes, 10 minutes, 15 minutes she sits, holding the milk-shake and crying, while Jamie and I murmur encouragingly.

Kitty, crying steadily, consumes the shake. Between bites she talks out loud to herself. She seems beyond caring that we can hear, or maybe she's so deep in her own nightmare that she doesn't know we're here.

'Come on, Kitty, you can do it,' she says. 'You don't want to go back to that scary place.' Jamie and I are crying now, too, as we understand for the first time exactly how courageous our daughter is. Each time she lifts the straw to her lips, her whole body shaking, she is jumping out of a plane at 30,000ft. Without a parachute.

## The Demonic Voice of an Eating Disorder

One afternoon about five days after Kitty comes home from hospital I'm sitting on the end of her bed, holding another protein milk-shake. Kitty sits propped up on pillows, crying. In the past half an hour I've managed to get three spoonfuls into her mouth.

She says she can't eat, she can't drink. She says her throat is closing, she's a horrible person, she's going to get fat, she's the worst person in the world. I sit on the end of her bed, stroking her foot, waiting for the tears to pass. I force myself to sit up, let a little edge slip into my tone. 'Kitty,' I say firmly, 'you have to drink this milk-shake. The doctor said so. Come on now, sit up. I'll get you a straw. It's melted anyway.'

Amazingly, Kitty sits up. She lifts her tear-streaked face towards me and I nearly drop the spoon. I know my daughter's face far better than I know my own. I know every look in her repertoire, but I've never seen this face before. Her eyes have gone blank; her mouth turns downward in almost a caricature of a pout. Her tongue pokes out, and for a second I think she's sticking it out at me.

Then I realise with horror that it's flicking like a snake's forked tongue. She opens her mouth, and her voice, too, is unrecognisable. She speaks in a singsongy, little-girl tone, the creepy voice of the witch in a fairytale. 'I'm a pig,' she says, not to me, exactly; it's almost like she's talking to herself. 'I'm a fat pig and I'm going to puke. I'm going to puke up everything because I'm such a pig.'

The hairs on the back of my neck stand up as the words pour from Kitty's mouth. No, not from Kitty's mouth, because this is not Kitty. It's not my daughter who looks out of those dead eyes, who rocks on the bed, her bone-arms wrapped around her flat chest, who says the same words over and over as if her brain was reduced to a single thought. It's as if a demon has possessed her. . . .

> **FAST FACT**
>
> A study led by Dr. James Lock found that a year after finishing treatment, 49 percent of teens receiving family-based treatment were in complete remission, compared with 23 percent of those given individual therapy.

## The Maudsley Approach

We decide to follow something called the Maudsley Approach, or family-based treatment, an approach that originated at the Maudsley Hospital in London. Rather than send Kitty away to a special facility, this means tackling the anorexia head on and together, in our home.

We consult with our paediatrician and then we make a plan. Jamie and I will take charge of Kitty's eating. We'll serve her breakfast, lunch, snack, dinner and snack, starting at about 1,500 calories a day, and we'll bump up the calories by 300 every couple of days, until she's getting enough. We will carry on like this—'refeeding' her—until she starts to gain weight.

The next morning Kitty comes downstairs to a bowl of cereal, milk and some strawberries. When she sees that the cereal is already in the bowl, that she doesn't get to measure it herself, her resistance begins.

Breakfast takes a full hour. Afterwards Kitty writhes on the living-room couch, crying, berating herself on and on for eating a whole bowl of cereal. I sit with her, stroke her hair and talk, words spilling out of me without thought or pause: 'I love you, you're my girl, you had no choice, I made you eat the cereal.'

We carefully monitor how many calories Kitty takes in and she has regular weigh-ins to make sure she's gaining weight. Day after day we live under the tyranny of the scales. After two weeks the numbers slowly start to rise.

## Living in a Bubble

Though Kitty is weighed 'blind,' with her back to the scales, she knows from our expressions. 'I gained weight! Oh my God!' she cries. She folds over on herself and begins a kind of moaning chant: 'I'm a fat pig, I'm gross and disgusting and lazy. Look what you're doing to me, you're making me fat. I should never have listened to you.'

For weeks we live in a kind of bubble. We see few friends, keep no social engagements. I've barely gone to the office; I've done the essentials of my job at home, late at night, after Kitty and Emma have gone to sleep. I'm usually too anxious to sleep, anyway. Our lives have narrowed to a few basic activities: shop, cook, eat, clean up, watch films, do it all again.

By the third week of September Kitty's weight has plateaued, so Jamie and I raise her calories to 3,500 a day. That's a lot of food. We go through so many packs of butter that I dream about unwrapping them in my sleep, peeling back the translucent paper, dropping them one by one into an enormous bowl.

Kitty's spirits have improved as her weight has inched up but the demon is still so close to the surface. One night, faced with a doughnut for her evening snack, Kitty begs for something different—a yogurt, toast, anything.

'You're trying to make me fat!' she says. 'This is disgusting. I feel greasy just looking at it. I can't eat this, it makes me feel sick.' On and on she goes. I stay calm, as I've learnt to. . . .

## Gradual Improvement

After that terrible year of refeeding things gradually got better. We let Kitty live away from home for the first time. She was 18, and part of the point of this was for her to become more independent. But three months later we brought her home after she relapsed, and began again the work of loosening the demon's claws.

One of the worst moments this time around came when Kitty confessed that, three years earlier, she'd sewed weights into a bra, and wore it every time we weighed her.

Kitty started college a term later than planned. She's not fully recovered from this relapse but she's made good progress. She knows that if she doesn't continue to recover we'll bring her home to finish the work here. Because the essential question remains the same now as it was four years ago: do we want her to have the life she was meant to have, full of colour and hope and joy? Or are we willing to settle for the grey half-life that comes from living with the demon?

The rest of the world may think we're being overprotective. We know the truth: we are saving our daughter's life, if not literally, then in every way that counts. We'll do whatever it takes to make sure Kitty gets well and stays well, whether she's 18 or 38. That's what families do.

# GLOSSARY

**amenorrhea**    The absence or suppression of a menstrual period.

**ana**    Slang for anorexia or anorexic.

**anorexia nervosa**    Medical term meaning "nervous loss of appetite," it is an eating disorder in which a person intentionally limits food intake to the point of emaciation and malnutrition, usually due to an abnormal fear of gaining weight.

**anosognosia**    An inability to recognize or take seriously one's illness.

**arrhythmia**    A disorder in the heart's normal rate or rhythmic beating.

**B&P**    An abbreviation for bingeing and purging.

**body dysmorphic disorder**    A disorder in which a person is preoccupied to the point of anxiety with his or her appearance, perceiving flaws in the face, hair, skin, and overall body shape.

**body image**    A person's subjective opinion about his or her physical appearance, such as shape, height, and weight. Body image is also based on the opinions and reactions of peers and family.

**body mass index**    A formula used to gauge a person's body fat based on a ratio of height to weight for each gender.

**bulimarexia**    A condition in which an individual cycles between anorexic and bulimic behaviors.

**bulimia nervosa**    Medical term meaning "ravenous hunger," it is an eating disorder in which an individual binges on food then purges the food from the body by self-induced vomiting, through the use of laxatives or enemas, or via excessive exercise.

**comorbid conditions**    The presence of one or more physical and/or mental conditions coexisting in a patient in addition to the patient's primary disease or disorder.

| | |
|---|---|
| dental caries | Also known as cavities, dental caries are holes in teeth from decay. People with bulimia are especially susceptible to caries because the stomach acid from excessive vomiting damages their teeth. |
| DSM | The *Diagnostic and Statistical Manual of Mental Disorders* (DSM) is published by the American Psychiatric Association and establishes the official diagnostic criteria for psychiatric conditions in North America. Currently in its revised fourth edition (DSM-IVR), with the next edition (DSM-V) scheduled for publication in 2013. |
| eating disorder | An illness in which an individual develops harmful eating patterns, typically by eating either too little or too much. Anorexia nervosa, bulimia nervosa, and binge eating are the most common types of eating disorders. |
| electrolyte imbalance | A physical condition in which the body has an imbalance in certain vital mineral ions, such as sodium, potassium, magnesium, and calcium, which in severe cases can lead to dehydration, cardiac arrest, organ failure, and death. People with bulimia tend to suffer electrolyte imbalance due to excessive vomiting. |
| emetic | A drug or substance, administered orally or by injection, that induces vomiting. People with bulimia use emetics to purge food from the body. |
| enema | The injection of liquid into the rectum for the purpose of evacuating the bowel. A common health practice, it is used by bulimics to purge food from the body. |
| hyperorexia | A synonym for bulimia. |
| hypoglycemia | Low blood sugar level. |
| ketosis | A medical condition characterized by an abnormal increase of ketones in the body, typically brought on by starvation, alcoholism, or diabetes. |
| lanugo | Fine, downy hair that can appear on the face or body of anorexics following an extreme loss of body fat. |
| mia | Slang for bulimia or bulimic. |

| | |
|---|---|
| obsessive-compulsive disorder | An anxiety disorder in which an individual experiences unwanted thoughts or obsessions and repetitive and compulsive behavior. |
| osteoporosis | A condition characterized by thinning bone tissue, a decrease in bone mass, that often leads to fractures. Osteoporosis, often caused by the lack of calcium, phosphorus, and protein, is a common complication of anorexia and bulimia. |
| refeeding syndrome | A dangerous and potentially fatal metabolic condition that can occur when nutrition is restored too quickly to a severely malnourished patient. |
| remission | The abatement or absence of the symptoms of a disease for a period of time. |
| Russell's sign | A symptom of bulimia or purge-type anorexia consisting of calluses on the back of one's hand or knuckles caused by repeated self-induced vomiting. |
| substance abuse | The misuse of alcohol or other drugs leading to impairment and lack of judgment. |
| thinspiration | A slang term used for photographs, poems, very thin models, or other material used to inspire and encourage young women to lose a lot of weight and become exceptionally thin. |
| trigger | A stimulus that initiates a reflex behavior or return to (or desire to return to) previous eating-disordered habits. |

# CHRONOLOGY

**A.D. 200–400**  Latin writings by Aulus Gellius and Sextus Pompeius Festus describe bulimic behavior.

**1200–1500**  During the Middle Ages, many women practice "holy anorexia," starving themselves to achieve mystical union with God.

**1398**  In the encyclopedia *De Proprietatibus Rerum* (*On the Order of Things*), English writer and translator John Trevisa describes "true boulimus" as a preoccupation with food followed by vomiting.

**1689**  In his *Phisiologia: A Treatise on Consumption*, British physician Richard Morton (1637–1698) describes the condition of anorexia nervosa.

**1694**  Morton reports the first case of anorexia in a sixteen-year-old man.

**1797**  *Bulimia* becomes an entry in the *Encyclopedia Britannica*.

**1859**  French physician Louis Victor Marce (1828–1864) is the first to publish a clinical account of a patient with anorexia nervosa.

**1873**  Charles Lasègue, a Paris neurologist, publishes "L'Anorexie hystérique," which focuses primarily on psychological aspects of the disorder; he considers it to be a condition that exclusively affects women.

**1873**  British physician Sir William Withey Gull (1819–1890) coins the term *anorexia nervosa* in a scientific paper he presents at a meeting of the Clinical Society of London and publishes in 1874. His work focuses more on physiological and nervous system aspects of the disorder and recognizes that it can affect men as well as women.

1926    At the Adult Weight Conference, a prominent physician reports a trend among young women of inducing vomiting after eating.

1932    In a paper for the German Psychoanalytic Society, Russian physician Moshe Wulff describes cases of eating disorders in women who binge eat, fast, vomit, and exhibit excessive sleepiness and irritability.

1932    *The New England Journal of Medicine* publishes the first photograph of a girl suffering from anorexia.

1945    In the post–World War II era, bulimia becomes more common as food again becomes plentiful and as society begins to admire slender celebrities.

1967    British model Twiggy (Lesley Hornby), at five feet seven and ninety-two pounds, initiates a trend toward excessive thinness.

1976    American counselor Marlene Boskind-White uses the word *bulimarexia* to describe women of normal weight who alternate between bingeing and fasting.

1978    Psychologist Hilde Bruch publishes *The Golden Cage*, a culmination of nearly thirty years of clinical experience with seventy patients suffering from anorexia nervosa.

1979    British professor Gerald Russell of Royal Free Hospital in London uses the term *bulimia nervosa* to recognize a variant syndrome of anorexia nervosa.

1980    The American Psychiatric Association recognizes bulimia nervosa as an autonomous eating disorder; previously it was considered a form of anorexia.

**1983**      Actress and fitness guru Jane Fonda reveals her history of bulimia, and popular singer Karen Carpenter dies from heart failure brought on by anorexia, raising public awareness of the disorders.

**1985**      The Renfrew Center in Philadelphia is the first free-standing facility dedicated exclusively to treating eating disorders.

**1986**      Ruth H. Strigel-Moore, Lisa R. Silberstein, and Judith Rodin publish the article "Toward an Understanding of Risk Factors for Bulimia" in *American Psychologist*, saying that female socialization is a contributing factor in bulimia.

**1989**      The US Congress designates a National Eating Disorders Awareness Week.

**1996**      Walter Kaye begins the first study, supported by the Price Foundation, to find a genetic link to eating disorders.

**late 1990s**      A pro–eating disorders movement forms on the World Wide Web, leading to attempts to censor or suppress it on the part of various organizations and governments.

**1999**      Harvard anthropologist Anne Becker and colleagues publish an influential study reporting that after the widespread introduction of television to Fiji, the percentage of subjects self-inducing vomiting to lose weight rose from 0 percent to 11 percent.

**2006**      Following several high-profile deaths of anorexic models such as Ana Carolina Reston, Spain and Italy ban the use of severely underweight models.

**2007**      A study from Harvard University reports that men comprise one in four cases of anorexia or bulimia, a much higher rate than previously thought.

2008    The Academy for Eating Disorders releases a position paper officially stating that anorexia and bulimia are to be considered "biologically based, serious mental illnesses."

2008    The US Congress passes the Mental Health Parity Law, which stipulates that people with eating disorders and other mental illnesses must receive insurance coverage equal to that provided for physical illnesses.

2008    Optenet, a computer security company, reports that pro-ana websites increased from 278 in 2006 to 1,583 in 2007, an increase of 470 percent.

2009    The federal Agency for Healthcare Research and Quality reports that hospitalizations for eating disorders declined by 23 percent between 2007–2009.

2010    The American Academy of Pediatrics releases a study reporting a 119 percent increase in eating disorder hospitalizations among children aged twelve or younger between 1999 and 2006.

2011    The British National Health Service reports that the number of men entering treatment for eating disorders is up by 66 percent.

2013    European neurological researchers find that anorexics have weak connections in the network of brain areas that process body image.

# ORGANIZATIONS TO CONTACT

The editors have compiled the following list of organizations concerned with the issues debated in this book. The descriptions are derived from materials provided by the organizations. All have publications or information available for interested readers. The list was compiled on the date of publication of the present volume; the information provided here may change. Be aware that many organizations take several weeks or longer to respond to inquiries, so allow as much time as possible.

**Academy for Eating Disorders (AED)**
111 Deer Lake Rd.,
Ste. 100
Deerfield, IL 60015
(847) 498-4274
fax: (847) 480-9282
website: www.aedweb
.org

The AED is a global multidisciplinary professional organization that provides cutting-edge professional training and education in eating disorders; inspires new developments in eating disorders research, prevention, and clinical treatments; and is the international source for state-of-the-art information in the field of eating disorders. The website's "Resources for the Public" section features videos providing information on eating disorders, ads requesting research study participants, and a directory of eating disorder professionals searchable by geographic area and other criteria.

**Alliance for Eating Disorders Awareness**
PO Box 2562
West Palm Beach, FL 33402
(866) 662-1235
e-mail: info@eating disordersinfo.org
website: www.alliance foreatingdisorders .com/

The Alliance for Eating Disorders Awareness was founded in the year 2000 as a source of community outreach, education, awareness, and prevention of anorexia, bulimia, and other eating disorders. It provides nationwide programs including presentations at public and private schools, professional training, and advocacy. Online offerings include information resources, referrals, and support groups.

**American Academy of Child and Adolescent Psychiatry (AACAP)**
3615 Wisconsin Ave. NW
Washington, DC 20016-3007
(202) 966-7300
e-mail: communica tions@aacap.org
website: www.aacap .org

AACAP is composed of child and adolescent psychiatrists who actively research, evaluate, diagnose, and treat psychiatric disorders, including anorexia and bulimia, as well as comorbid disorders. Entering "eating disorders" in the website's search bar yields hundreds of results.

**American Psychiatric Association (APA)**
1000 Wilson Blvd, Ste. 1825
Arlington, VA 22209
(888) 357-7924
e-mail: apa@psych.org
website: www.psych .org

The APA is an organization of psychiatrists dedicated to study-ing the nature, treatment, and prevention of mental disorders, including those that contribute to eating disorders. The APA helps create mental health policies, distributes information about psychiatry, and promotes psychiatric research and educa-tion. It also publishes the *Diagnostic and Statistical Manual of Mental Disorders* and a number of journals, and by way of the "Mental Health" tab on its website, visitors can access bro-chures and other information on specific topics.

**American Psychological Association (APA)**
750 First St. NE
Washington, DC 20002-4242
(202) 336-5500; toll-free: (800) 374-2721
e-mail: public.affairs @apa.org
website: www.apa.org

The APA is a scientific and professional organization represent-ing psychology in the United States. With 150,000 members, APA is the largest association of psychologists worldwide. It publishes several journals, including *American Psychologist*, and produces numerous publications on eating disorders and related matters.

**Anorexia Nervosa and Related Eating Disorders, Inc. (ANRED)**
PO Box 5102
Eugene, OR 97405
(503) 344-1144
website: www.anred
.com

ANRED is a nonprofit organization that provides information about anorexia nervosa, bulimia nervosa, binge-eating disorder, compulsive exercising, and other lesser-known food and weight disorders, including details about recovery and prevention. ANRED offers workshops, individual and professional training, forums for discussion, as well as local community education.

**Eating Disorders Anonymous (EDA)**
PO Box 55876
Phoenix, AZ 85078-5876
e-mail: info@eating
disordersanonymous
.org
website: www.eating
disordersanonymous
.org

EDA is a fellowship of individuals who share their experiences, strengths, and hopes with each other with the goal of solving their common problems and helping others to recover from their eating disorders. Members of EDA identify and claim milestones of recovery. The only requirement for membership is a desire to recover from an eating disorder. There are no dues or fees for EDA membership. The website offers recovery resources, a list of meetings, and a chatroom that also hosts online meetings.

**Eating Disorders Coalition for Research, Policy, and Action (EDC)**
720 Seventh St. NW, Ste. 300
Washington, DC 20001
(202) 543-9570
e-mail: manager@
eatingdisorderscoali
tion.org
website: www.eating
disorderscoalition.org

The EDC is a cooperative of professional and advocacy-based organizations committed to advocacy on behalf of people with eating disorders, their families, and professionals working with these populations. The mission of the EDC is to advance the federal government's recognition of eating disorders as a public health priority. The EDC blog provides updates on related news and opportunities for individuals to get involved.

**Jessie's Wish**
742 Colony Forest
Dr.,
Midlothian, VA 23114
(804) 378-3032
e-mail: jessieswish
@verizon.net
website: www.jessies
wish.org

Jessie's Wish is a nonprofit organization that seeks to help individuals suffering from eating disorders, and their families, by providing education on the devastating effects of anorexia, bulimia, and other eating disorders and by helping with financial assistance when health insurance is inadequate or unavailable.

**The Joy Project**
PO Box 16488
St. Paul, MN 55116
e-mail: info@joy
project.org
website: www.joy
project.org

The Joy Project is a nonprofit, grassroots organization based on the philosophy of using real-world, workable solutions to end the epidemic of eating disorders. It works toward reducing the rate and severity of eating disorders by supporting and conducting research, education, and support programs. The website offers recovery resources and news on events.

**Multi-Service Eating Disorders Association (MEDA)**
92 Pearl St., Newton,
MA 02458
(617) 558-1881
e-mail: info@medainc
.org
website: www.medainc
.org

The MEDA is a nonprofit organization dedicated to the prevention and treatment of eating disorders and disordered eating. The association's mission is to prevent the continuing spread of eating disorders through educational awareness and early detection. MEDA serves as a support network and resource for clients, loved ones, clinicians, educators, and the general public. The MEDA website features a signup for its monthly e-newsletter, opportunities to get involved, and informational resources and links.

**National Association of Anorexia and Associated Disorders (ANAD)**
800 E. Diehl Road #160
Naperville, IL 60563
(630) 577-1330
e-mail: anadhelp@anad.org
website: www.anad.org

ANAD offers hotline counseling and an online forum, operates an international network of support groups for people with eating disorders and their families, and provides referrals to health-care professionals who treat eating disorders. It produces a quarterly newsletter and information packets and organizes national conferences and local programs. All ANAD services are provided free of charge.

*National Eating Disorder Information Center (NEDIC)*
ES 7-421, 200 Elizabeth St.
Toronto, ON M5G 2C4
CANADA
(866) 633-4220
e-mail: nedic@uhn.ca
website: www.nedic.ca

NEDIC provides information and resources on eating disorders and weight preoccupation. It focuses on the sociocultural factors that influence female health-related behaviors. NEDIC promotes healthy lifestyles and encourages individuals to make informed choices using accurate information. It publishes a newsletter and a guide for families and friends of eating-disorder sufferers and sponsors Eating Disorders Awareness Week in Canada.

**National Eating Disorders Association (NEDA)**
165 W. Forty-Sixth St.
New York, NY 10036
(212) 575-6200
e-mail: info@nationaleatingdisorders.org
website: www.nationaleatingdisorders.org

NEDA is the largest nonprofit organization in the United States working to prevent eating disorders and provide treatment referrals to those suffering from anorexia, bulimia, and binge-eating disorders and those concerned with body image and weight issues. NEDA also provides educational outreach programs and training for schools and universities. The organization publishes a prevention curriculum for grades four through six as well as public prevention and awareness information packets, audio and video resources, guides, and other materials.

**National Eating Disorders Screening Program (NEDSP)**
One Washington St., Ste. 304
Wellesley Hills, MA 02481
(781) 239-0071
fax: (781) 431-7447
e-mail: smhinfo@ mentalhealthscreen ing.org
website: www.mental healthscreening.org /events/national-eat ing-disorder-screening -program.aspx

The NEDSP focuses on anorexia nervosa, bulimia nervosa, and binge-eating disorder. The goal of the program is to raise the level of awareness about eating disorders and to encourage people who may be suffering from eating disorders to seek further help and treatment. The program provides in-person and online programs for eating disorders implemented by local clinicians at mental health facilities, hospitals, primary-care offices, social service agencies, colleges and universities, workplaces, schools, and the military.

# FOR FURTHER READING

**Books**

Stephanie Covington Armstrong, *Not All Black Girls Know How to Eat: A Story of Bulimia.* Chicago: Lawrence Hill, 2009.

Carrie Arnold and B. Timothy Walsh, *Next to Nothing: A Firsthand Account of One Teenager's Experience with an Eating Disorder.* Oxford: Oxford University Press, 2007.

Harriet Brown, ed., *Feed Me! Writers Dish About Food, Eating, Weight, and Body Image.* New York: Ballantine, 2009.

Joan Jacobs Brumberg, *Fasting Girls: The History of Anorexia Nervosa.* New York: Vintage, 2000.

Pamela Carlton and Deborah Ashin, *Take Charge of Your Child's Eating Disorder: A Physician's Step-by-Step Guide to Defeating Anorexia and Bulimia.* New York: Marlowe, 2007.

Shannon Cutts, *Beating ANA: How to Outsmart Your Eating Disorder and Take Your Life Back.* Deerfield Beach, FL: Health Communications, 2009.

Lesli J. Favor and Kira Freed, *Food as Foe: Nutrition and Eating Disorders.* New York: Marshall Cavendish Benchmark, 2010.

Peach Friedman, *Diary of an Exercise Addict.* Guilford, CT: GPP Life, 2008.

Gary A. Grahl, *Skinny Boy: A Young Man's Battle and Triumph Over Anorexia.* Clearfield, UT: American Legacy Media, 2007.

Barbara Hale-Seubert, *Riptide: Struggling with and Resurfacing from a Daughter's Eating Disorder.* Toronto: ECW, 2011.

Lindsey Hall and Leigh Conn, *Bulimia: A Guide to Recovery.* New York: Gürze, 2010.

Sheila Himmel and Lisa Himmel, *Hungry: A Mother and Daughter Fight Anorexia.* New York: Berkley, 2009.

Sandra J. Judd, *Eating Disorders Sourcebook.* 3rd ed. Detroit: Omnigraphics, 2011.

Aimee Liu, ed., *Restoring Our Bodies, Reclaiming Our Lives: Guidance and Reflections on Recovery from Eating Disorders.* Boston: Trumpeter, 2011.

Jena Morrow, *Hollow: An Unpolished Tale.* Chicago: Moody, 2010.

Tamra Orr, *When the Mirror Lies: Anorexia, Bulimia, and Other Eating Disorders.* Danbury, CT: Franklin Watts, 2007.

Lisa M. Schab, *The Bulimia Workbook for Teens: Activities to Help You Stop Bingeing and Purging.* Oakland, CA: Instant Help Books, 2010.

Sari Fine Shepphird, *101 Questions & Answers About Anorexia Nervosa.* Sudbury, MA: Jones and Bartlett, 2010.

Michele Siegel, Judith Brisman, and Margot Weinshel, *Surviving an Eating Disorder: Strategies for Families and Friends.* 3rd ed. New York: Collins Living, 2009.

Kate Taylor, ed., *Going Hungry: Writers on Desire, Self-denial, and Overcoming Anorexia.* New York: Anchor, 2008.

## Periodicals and Internet Sources

Rondi Adamson, "Fashionistas: Go Big? Or Go Home?," *Globe & Mail* (Toronto), January 23, 2007.

June Alexander, "No Eating Disorder Is an Island," JuneAlexander.com, November 3, 2012. www.junealexander.com/2012/03/no-eating-disorder-is-an-island.

Diana Appleyard, "Anorexia Almost Killed Me Too But I Was Cured by Horses," *Daily Express* (London), May 4, 2012. www.express.co.uk/posts/view/318108/Anorexia-almost-killed-me-too-but-I-was-cured-by-horses.

Elizabeth Nolan Brown, "Eating Disorder Lit: Helpful or Triggering?," Blisstree, February 29, 2012. http://blisstree.com/feel/eating-disorder-memoirs-and-books-helpful-or-triggering-910.

Harriet Brown, "A Mother's Plea to Shut the 'Hunger Blogs,'" *Huffington Post*, February 15, 2012. www.huffingtonpost.com/harriet-brown/a-mothers-plea-to-shut-the-_b_1277082.html.

Chanel Dubofsky, "Anorexic Teens Get (the Reality TV) Treatment," *Sisterhood* (blog), January 4, 2012. http://blogs.forward.com/sisterhood-blog/149014/anorexic-teens-get-the-reality-tv-treatment.

Vanessa D. Fisher, "The Untouchables—My Descent into Hell and What It Taught Me About Beauty," *Reflections* (blog), July 22, 2012. www.vanessadfisher.com/blog/beauty-the-existential-beast-my-descent-into-ugliness.

Chrissie Giles, "A Burst from the Blue: Is Bulimia Nervosa Really a Modern Disease?," Wellcome Trust, February 20, 2012. www.wellcome.ac.uk/News/2012/Features/WTVM054405.htm.

Shari Graydon, "'Disordered Eating' Is Still a Beauty of a Problem," *Globe & Mail* (Toronto), March 31, 2010.

Emanuella Grinberg, "Sex, Lies and Media: New Wave of Activists Challenge Notions of Beauty," CNN, March 9, 2012. http://articles.cnn.com/2012-03-09/living/living_beauty-media-miss-representation_1_social-media-natural-beauty-jennifer-siebel-newsom?_s=PM:LIVING.

Meredith Lepore, "My Job Is My Bulimia Trigger," Grindstone, February 28, 2012. http://thegrindstone.com/work-life-balance/my-job-is-my-bulimia-trigger-288.

Aimee Liu, "Moving from an Eating Disorder's Half-Life to Your Full Life," *Huffington Post*, January 18, 2012. www.huffingtonpost.com/aimee-liu/eating-disorder-treatment_b_1195009.html.

Rebekah McAlinden, "The Reality of Anorexia & Bulimia," *R is for Recovery (and Rebekah)* (blog), March 28, 2012. http://risforrecovery.wordpress.com/2012/03/28/the-reality-of-anorexia-bulimia.

Medusa, "Anorexia, Bulimia, & the Minnesota Starvation Experiment," August 10, 2009. www.2medusa.com/2009/08/anorexia-bulimia-minnesota-starvation.html.

Abigail Natenshon, "When Parents Have Eating Disorders," Empowered Parents, n.d. www.empoweredparents.com/1parentsissues/parents_01.htm.

Hanna Brooks Olson, "True Story: I've Been Using Pro-ana Websites for over a Decade," Blisstree, March 2, 2012. http://blisstree.com/look/ive-used-pro-ana-websites-for-12-years-961/#ixzz22ufG4SNj.

Jemima Owen, "In Focus: Viewpoint: 'In the Real World I Was Lost to Anorexia, but Online the Kindness of 1,500 Strangers a Day Helped Save My Life," *Observer* (London), March 27, 2011.

Elizabeth P., "Recovering from an Eating Disorder in Today's Weight-centric Society," Psych Central, June, 2011. http://blogs.psychcentral.com/weightless/2011/06/recovering-from-an-eating-disorder-in-todays-weight-centric-society.

Elizabeth Palmberg, "Body Language," *Sojourners*, April, 2009.

Nathaniel Penn, "20% of Anorexics Are Men," *GQ*, September 2012.

Andrew Pollack, "Eating Disorders a New Front in Insurance Fight," *New York Times,* October 14, 2011.

Rachel Richardson, "Dieting, Repackaged," *The-F-Word* (blog), July 2, 2009. http://the-f-word.org/blog/index.php/2009/07/02/dieting-repackaged.

Shari Roan, "Experts See Hopeful Signs on Eating Disorders," *Los Angeles Times*, April 17, 2012. http://articles.latimes.com/2012/apr/17/health/la-he-eating-disorders-20120417.

Carolyn Coker Ross, "Is Unresolved Trauma Preventing a Full Eating Disorder Recovery?," Psych Central, March 5, 2012. http://psychcentral.com/blog/archives/2012/03/05/is-unresolved-trauma-preventing-a-full-eating-disorder-recovery.

Fred Schwarz, "The Daisy Duke Diet," *National Review*, February 17, 2009.

Maia Szalavitz, "A Genetic Link Between Anorexia and Autism?," *Time*, June 19, 2009.

Margarita Tartakovsky, "Body Image, Bullying & Eating Disorders in the Gay Community," Psych Central, December 15, 2011. http://blogs.psychcentral.com/weightless/2011/12/body-image-bullying-eating-disorders-in-the-gay-community.

———, "The Stigma of Eating Disorders & Setting Stereotypes Straight," PsychCentral, May 18, 2011. http://blogs.psychcentral.com/weightless/2011/05/the-stigma-of-eating-disorders-setting-stereotypes-straight.

Lance Workman, "The Evolution of Eating Disorders," *Psychology Review,* September, 2009.

Kareen Wynter, "Opinion: The Dangers of Labels, and How They Contributed to My Bulimia," CNN, March 22, 2012. http://inamerica.blogs.cnn.com/2012/03/22/opinion-the-dangers-of-labels-and-how-they-contributed-to-my-bulimia.

# INDEX